Randolph S. Foster

Philosophy of Christian Experience

eight lectures delivered before the Ohio Wesleyan University on the Merrick

Foundation. Third Series

Randolph S. Foster

Philosophy of Christian Experience

eight lectures delivered before the Ohio Wesleyan University on the Merrick Foundation. Third Series

ISBN/EAN: 9783337238773

Printed in Europe, USA, Canada, Australia, Japan

Cover: Foto ©Thomas Meinert / pixelio.de

More available books at **www.hansebooks.com**

PHILOSOPHY OF

CHRISTIAN EXPERIENCE

EIGHT LECTURES

DELIVERED BEFORE THE OHIO WESLEYAN UNIVERSITY

ON THE MERRICK FOUNDATION

BY

RANDOLPH S. FOSTER

THIRD SERIES

NEW YORK: HUNT & EATON
CINCINNATI: CRANSTON & STOWE
1891

Copyright, 1890, by
HUNT & EATON,
NEW YORK.

PREFACE.

THE honored projector of the foundation under whose auspices the following lectures were delivered—himself a ripe scholar, a venerable and venerated teacher, a beautiful exponent of Christian character—still lives. The foundation provides for "*an annual course of at least five lectures on Experimental and Practical Religion.*" It is doubtful whether, pressed as the lecturer was, at the time he received the invitation to deliver one of the courses, with other uncompleted and weighty literary engagements in addition to onerous official duties, and withal not over strong, he could have entertained the suggestion for a moment, but for two circumstances.

The first of these circumstances was, that, unconsciously, and probably wholly unknown to himself, the founder of the lectureship had been for more than fifty years a constructive force in the mind life and spiritual life of the lecturer. It is not given us to know here what subtle influences go from us, fashioning other lives. Possibly it may be an element of the joy or sorrow of eternity to make the discovery. It gives me profound pleasure to make this public acknowledgment of a long-standing debt of gratitude. The pressure of a hand laid on me when a stripling is still sensibly felt.

The second circumstance that moved me to consent was the theme suggested, "The Philosophy of Christian Experience." Had the matter of selecting a subject been left to myself, it is probable preoccupancy with other great discussions would have been a formidable if not fatal hinderance. The mind already tense with uncompleted investigations does not readily adjust itself to the search for new lines. The offered theme opened an inviting door. The task was accepted. The lectures to follow are the result.

The subject is sympathetic with the temper of the age. It deals with facts rather than speculations; with experimental verities rather than mere dogmas. It subjects Christianity to practical tests, and so puts it in line with scientific method. It offers the inner experiences of the soul to the examination and explanation of reason. The age busies itself with facts, demands facts, will have nothing but facts, relegates all speculation; the subject accepts the situation, and presents facts for consideration—the deepest and most indisputable of all facts: not the mere facts of sense, about which there may be dispute and which relate to merely material and temporal things, but the deeper facts of the soul, facts of consciousness, about which it is impossible there should be any dispute; facts which affect character and destiny, therefore of the most profound interest possible.

CONTENTS.

LECTURE I.
LIMITATIONS AND DEFINITIONS.................................... 5

LECTURE II.
IMPLICATIONS AND CONDITIONING GROUNDS OF EXPERIENCE............... 26

LECTURE III.
ANTECEDENT HISTORY AND PRINCIPLES WHICH COLOR EXPERIENCE......... 49

LECTURE IV.
PROCESS AND ELEMENTS OF EXPERIENCE. FORGIVENESS.................. 74

LECTURE V.
ELEMENTS OF EXPERIENCE CONTINUED. REGENERATION................... 86

LECTURE VI.
FACTS WHICH CONDITION EXPERIENCE SUBSEQUENT TO REGENERATION...... 109

LECTURE VII.
SOME PHASES OF EXPERIENCE....................................... 127

LECTURE VIII.
POSSIBILITIES OF GRACE, AND ADVICES............................. 154

PHILOSOPHY OF
CHRISTIAN EXPERIENCE.

LECTURE I.
LIMITATIONS AND DEFINITIONS.

The greatest difficulty I have found in preparing these lectures has been to determine what things to exclude so as to bring them within allowed limits; and yet so as not to mar them by leaving out matters which ought to be mentioned, as having essential bearings on the subject to be discussed. An attempt to give a philosophy of Christian experience without discussing the doctrine of human sin and sinfulness, for instance, seems to be commencing to build in the air; the same is true of the doctrine of atonement; yet any one at all informed on the nature of these subjects and of the breadth of discussion they involve will see that either of them, to be discussed at all, would require more than all the time I have for my entire subject. It is impossible, therefore, for me to enter the field of polemics on these points at all. They are fully discussed in *Studies in Theology*, now going through the press. The only possible attention I can give them in these lectures is the briefest reference and simple statement when continuity of thought demands it.

The stand-point from which the discussion proceeds is, broadly, that occupied by Arminian theologians, without slavish adherence to all the incidents put into the theory by many of its advocates. Its theory of sin and atonement and cognate doctrines is assumed as substantially correct, without any attempt at unfolding or defending the positions held. But, while this is the stand-point which my mind holds theologically, it must be kept in mind that I have no concern whatever about the defense of any theological system. I am not proposing to treat the subject theologically at all, and am utterly careless about systems as such. My line is entirely another—deals with facts and the philosophy of them.

It is proper to say, before entering upon the discussion to which these lectures are to be devoted, that they do not propose a philosophy of religion, or even a philosophy of the Christian system of religion. These are cognate and generally related subjects to our topic, but are broader, and our limits will not permit us even to broach them. There are many able treatises on these distinct topics within the reach of every student, which, in order to the best theological furnishing, ought to be read and studied with care. As an invaluable treatise of this kind, bearing directly on Christian apologetics, I commend Walker's *Philosophy of the Plan of Salvation;* in many respects equal, and in some respects superior, to Bishop Butler's masterpiece, *The Analogy of Religion, Natural and Revealed, to the Constitution and Course of Nature*, which, of course, no student is unacquainted with. I also commend, as of great value, the two works of Dr. Mark Hopkins, *Lectures on Moral Philosophy and Ethics*, and *The Law of Love and Love a Law;* likewise Bushnell's *Nature and the Supernatural.* And I will venture to speak of yet one other, which I have been permitted to see in manuscript, for which the world has been waiting too long, and I hope may not have to wait much longer, *Comparative Religions*, by Dr. William F. Warren, of the Boston University.

These lectures will be strictly limited to the investigation of "the philosophy of Christian experience." There have been many works written on the subject of Christian experience, some practical and experimental, some speculative, critical, and theological, but, so far as I am informed, while many of these have been stimulating and helpful to thought none have attempted a philosophy of the subject. We enter, therefore, upon a somewhat new and, in some respects, unfinger-boarded and untrodden way. It is proper I should say that our path lies broad away from a strictly biblical or theological treatise; and from hortation or an attempt to stimulate to the pursuit of an experience. I propose no theological polemic. For my purposes I shall make the least possible reference theologizing. Nor will it be expected that I shall deal with matters of exegesis. As nearly as possible I will omit any reference to the text. This may seem strange in treating of such a theme as Christian experience, but it is precisely what my thesis demands. I am to deal with matters of experience—purely subjective phenomena ; to inquire what they are, and how they are to be explained. Theological and biblical principles are involved and will emerge, but they do not enter into my discussion directly. No position taken will depend for its support or will be supported by appeal to the Bible, though some will depend on the Bible for their historical grounds.

Perhaps it ought to be stated more explicitly that the method pursued in this discussion is entirely different from that ordinarily pursued in dealing with Christian topics. The usual method is to attempt to find what is taught in or deduceable from the Bible. The book is court of final resort; its dictum is decisive. The aim is to find what it teaches. Now this is not my aim at all. I do not even raise the question. My point is to find what human experience is, and what human experience teaches along certain lines. This will explain why so little reference is made to the Bible in these lectures.. Other treatises—

a former treatise of my own—proceed from the view-point of the Bible. This discussion is from the view-point of the soul itself.

This course is pursued as the only legitimate course in essaying to give a philosophy of facts which are wholly facts of experience. I desire attention to every position taken, and hold myself under obligation to the proof that nothing advanced is contrary to the word of God when the proof is demanded. My hope is to show that Christian experience is capable of rational interpretation and defense ; and so to make it appear that concrete Christianity, or the Christianity of experience, rationally unfolded, is precisely the Christianity of the Bible, doctrinally revealed.

Some of the positions taken will impinge on current systems, and some opinions about them will be expressed, but only as they bear on the philosophy propounded, not at all on the theological polemic.

The demand for definition. What is definition ? The terms of the thesis call for definition. Definition itself needs to be defined. It is essential to definition that it define ; that is, that it should separate the object defined from every other subject, so that it becomes a distinct object of thought—set off by itself. That is the etymological significance of the term—to bound, or set boundaries. Nothing approaches definition that does not secure this first condition. But this is not sufficient. Definition must include all that is essential to the object defined. If any essential is left out, the definition falls short of its aim in an essential point, and the defect may be such as to involve utter error. The statement of the most important fact, with respect to an object, is not a definition of it, though it may indicate it. The definition must include every essential and exclude every thing else. If more is put into the definition than is included in the thing defined, the object is not before the mind, but some other object—a distortion. The included error may be such as to be utterly misleading and involve fatal misdirection.

Truth is exact, and to reach it the utmost possible precision is necessary in the use of significant terms ; never more so than in a discussion like the present. General statements, when all their inclusions are fully understood and mutually accepted, may so indicate an object as to preclude the necessity of more formal and elaborate definition, but when the subject is one of fundamental importance, and there are possible diverse views, such general statements are always to be looked upon with suspicion, and create a demand for examination lest some covert meaning having in it concealed error be intended, or, if not intended, be nevertheless introduced. It is not an uncommon thing for error to be so masked in plausible general terms as to impose upon those who use them, as well as those addressed by them. They have such a semblance to truth, and in some instances so manifestly contain *a* truth, that, while containing along with the truth a fatal error, the error is so concealed as not to be discovered, and the truth itself is made to give currency to a destructive falsehood. It is in this way that the most damaging systems of error gain foothold with honest minds. Error never comes naked. It drapes itself in garbs of truth and thus insidiously insinuates and establishes itself. It is a rogue which, knowing that if seen alone it would not be tolerated for a moment, always comes in a crowd of well-known respectable truths, and seeks to gain admission by the good company it keeps. It is by this subtlety that false systems of doctrine and heretical creeds always put as much truth in them as possible, and give these truths prominence, and call themselves by old and honored names, that under these disguises they may inject their poison without starting apprehension.

Philosophy. By philosophy we understand the knowledge and rational explanation of phenomena as to their causes and significance. The term has been variously defined as "The science of things divine and human, and the causes in which they are contained;" "the science of effects and their causes;" "the science of the sufficient reason;" "the science of things deduced from first principles." All these definitions are of the same general import, and, more simply construed, signify that by the term philosophy is meant the understanding and explanation of phenomena of which the mind becomes aware either by observation or consciousness; as to their causes, laws, and significance.

To render a philosophy of any subject is simply to give a sufficiently full statement of the facts and contents of the subject, and furnish a rational, that is, an intelligible and adequate, explanation of them. To know a thing and not know its causal grounds is imperfect knowledge—next door to absolute ignorance—and opens the mind to all sorts of fancies and superstitions. To know a thing and also know its causes is enlarged knowledge, and closes the door of the mind against a mob of delusions, but does not furnish it perfect content. There remains still the question, for what?—or, what does it signify? to what end is it? When an object is known as to what it is, and as to its cause, how it is, or by what power it is, and when additionally it is known as to why it is, for what end it is, we have reached true knowledge—science—philosophy. This by a law of the mind is its everlasting search; until the attainment is reached it can have no fruition of content. It is the goal of rational existence.

Experience. The term experience is thus defined by Webster: "Particular acquaintance with any matter by personal observation or trial of it; by feeling its effects; by living through it." It is thus made the equivalent of personal knowledge of external facts and things, by perceiving them or by observation of any kind; and of all internal states of feeling which emerge in consciousness, whether intellectual, emotional, or volitional. This is a broad use of the term; and it may be doubted whether for strict accuracy it is not too broad. There would seem to be a sufficient difference between matters of observation and matters of consciousness not to class them as identical. The one relates to matters objective, the other to matters subjective. The objective offers itself to experiment, the subjective to experience. Experience more specifically relates to the internal states and feelings, existing as present, or recalled as past, consciousnesses, through which one has passed or is passing. This is the sense in which it is more commonly used and in which it is invariably used in these lectures.

Whatever a man experiences he knows. It is the knowing that constitutes the experience. If he did not know the experience he could not be said to have it. There is no consciousness of which we are not conscious or of which we have not knowledge.

In this discussion I am to be employed specifically about facts—subjective states and feelings which emerge in consciousness; therefore the most immediate and indisputable matters of knowledge. Theories, dogmas, speculative inference as to facts themselves have no place. Consciousness furnishes them. They do not require proof. The experience is the proof. They will admit of no other. The proof of pain is that we feel it. The same is true of all subjective experiences. The proof of them is that we have them.

The philosophy of these matters of experience comprises simply the consciousness of them, the right understanding of their grounds and sources and their significance, or relation to ends to be served by them.

This exhausts the subject, and leaves nothing further to place them in the line of rational or understood knowledges. We cannot explain how the soul receives subjective impressions. Consciousness itself is a final fact, and admits of no explanation. The furthest possible point to which we can push inquiry as to the facts themselves which emerge in consciousness is to find them and their causes, and the ends they serve. Many times we are compelled to stop short of this. We can simply know the facts. In such cases the philosophy of the facts remains impossible. If we can go further, and find how it is that the facts exist and any ends which they are manifestly intended to serve, we have the entire philosophy of them.

If we choose to use the term experience in the broadest sense as including matters of personal observation, then there is a difference between an experience of Christianity and a Christian experience. An experience of Christianity is the result of personal observation as to its effects on individuals, peoples, and institutions, its moral and social tendencies, how it affects welfare in respect of education, industrial habits, commercial ethics, and all things that enter into the general improvement and happiness of communities. One who by living with it has become acquainted with it so as to have knowledge of it on these points may be said to have experience of Christianity—he has seen and felt its workings. There is yet a deeper experience than these general effects of the system felt by many—in personal influences which reach them through its teachings, which consciously modify their thoughts, feeling, moral habits, and principles, and personal character—who yet have no Christian experience, but only experience of some Christian influences; who are not, and well know themselves not to be, Christians. The experience in both these kinds indicates something of what Christianity is, and is of high apologetical value. It points to a power for good in the system which the world needs, and, so, broadly indicates its probable truth; and where the experience is all one way, as, we are bold to say, it always is, condemns revilers on their own experience. But it is not an experience of this kind that we seek to illuminate—its matters do not emerge in our thesis in any form.

It is worth while to observe further on this matter of experience that, while matters of experience are relatively the clearest and most satisfactory among our knowledges, things about which we affirm with the greatest assurance that we do absolutely know, they are knowledges of which we can convey no adequate conception to minds that are wholly out of the plane of the experience. The language of experience is intelligible only to those who have something in common by which to interpret it. I was never so impressed with this fact and its importance as during the preparation of these lectures. Certain passages of Scripture have come to have an emphasis of meaning which I had not before discovered in them: "The natural man receiveth [or knoweth] not the things of the Spirit of God: for they are foolishness unto him: neither *can* he know them, for they are spiritually discerned;" "It is given unto you to know the mysteries of the kingdom of heaven, but to them [that are without] it is not given;" "Except a man be born again [or born from above], he *cannot* see [or discern] the kingdom of God;" "If I have told you earthly things, and ye believed not, how shall ye believe if I tell you of heavenly things?" The import of which is, spiritual experiences cannot be apprehended by an unspiritualized mind. To speak of them to such is to speak in a practically unknown tongue. The spiritual man lives in a world of spiritual things which to him is perfectly plain, but which is wholly foreign to an unspiritualized mind. Some things all minds have in common concerning which they are mutually intelligible to each other; but the spiritual man has entered a realm which is foreign to his unspiritual friend, and when he speaks of it there is nothing common between them to interpret his meaning—his speech is unintelligible. This is so important that I dwell for its further illustration. When two men understand the same language, so long as they converse together in it they are intelligible to each other; but if one of the two knows a language which the other does not, and he commences to use that, all connection is cut off between them as completely as if they had nothing in common. It is so when one speaks of an experience of which the other has no analogous experience. He may employ a language every term of which is understood, but he cannot make himself intelligible. Take two men, one of whom is blind. Both have perfect use of the same language, and on most subjects they converse intelligibly to each other; but on one subject speech to the blind man becomes utterly unintelligible, meaningless: the subject of color. To understand the meaning of that term he must have what he has not—eyes. Without eyes he is left to mere conjecture. To the one who has eyes nothing is plainer, and to those who have eyes no speech is more intelligible than that which relates to color. It is easy to convey the idea of the minutest shades of difference in colors. The same rule applies to flavors, sounds, and, indeed, all matters of sensation. It is no less applicable to matters merely subjective—matters of consciousness. In order to intelligibility there must be something in common.

Mutual experiences make mutual intelligibility under the greatest embarrassments. The soul has many languages through which it communicates to kindred souls—not one through which it can communicate with a soul wholly alien to it. Put a spiritualized soul, whose only speech-language is English, in a congregation of spiritualized German souls, and let the exercises of hymn and prayer and sermon and sacrament and testimony be all in the unknown tongue, the spiritualized English soul will not be a foreigner; there will be, intoning the unintelligible jargon of unmeaning sounds, something which it understands—the language of face and feature and tearful eye and voice which translates itself by the magic of a common experience—and the sympathetic souls will recognize each other. But they can only interpret each other by a common experience. An unspiritual mind is dead to spiritual things. It walks among them, but does not discern them; it hears of them, but the language is unintelligible.

It is because of this law that we find it impossible, even under the highest spiritual experiences, to form any satisfactory conception of heavenly things, heavenly beings, their modes of life and communication among themselves. Every one who has attempted to think along these lines is conscious of the difficulty. The explanation is, the experiences are out of our plane—there is not enough in common between us to enable us to form a conception except of the most general kind, and even of such conceptions it is impossible to know how much, if any, truth there is in them. The highest certainty we can reach is that there is a spiritual world comprising divers orders and grades of life, from the Infinite to the most recent and infantile spirit, and that their life is the most exalted. We are wholly unable to fill out or interpret these general phrases, simply because they are out of our plane and our earthly experience has so little in common with them. In like manner and for the same reason are the experiences of a spiritualized soul unintelligible to an unspiritualized soul. Their planes are in this respect uneven—without correspondence. What is perfectly intelligible to the one is not intelligible to the other; what moves the one does not move the other; what appeals to the one does not appeal to the other.

Christian experiences are the experiences of a soul in a fallen world; that is, the plane in which it lives and by which all its experiences are modified. Its experiences interpret nothing out of its plane. What the experiences of Adam would have been had he not sinned, and become sensualized, for this reason we can but very imperfectly conceive. So far as there was in the plane of his life any thing in common with the life we live we find it not difficult to form a sufficiently clear conception. The general effect of the external world upon him; his physical sensations; his love for Eve; his round of daily employment in tilling the garden; his growth of knowledge—things of this kind, we fancy, there is enough in common between his life and ours to put us *en rapport*, so that we get, as we suppose, a tolerable understanding of his experiences in these respects. But when we attempt to pass beyond this, and try to think of his subjective consciousnesses, or what they would have been had he not sinned, and the kind of man they would have made of him, we find ourselves in a plane which we cannot travel—our guides forsake us. What the daily pabulum of a sinless soul in a sinless world would be we do not know; we have nothing by which to interpret. We are so accustomed to tainted air that we can hardly imagine respiration possible in any other; so used to the contact of evil, its absolute enswathement every moment, that we cannot conceive life going on without it. We are so used to conflict and trouble growing out of sin that we find it difficult to conceive what would be the use and function of a life in a world where sin did not exist. The experiences of an unsinning and unsinful soul going forward through a life-time in a world which the blight of sin had never reached, in which nothing existed that came of sin, in which all things were in holy harmony; the experiences of such a soul so insphered, I suspect, if recited to us would find in us as little response as a recitation in an unknown dialect, it would have so much in it above our comprehension.

It ought to be noted yet further that every experience is colored by the subject of the experience. I mean by this that precisely the same experience reports itself differently in minds of dissimilar temperaments, degrees of intelligence, antecedent habits, prejudices, preconceptions, education, and ruling ideas. This fact must be taken account of in dealing with Christian experience. The subjects of Christian experience are extremely various.

It is customary to lump Christians in a class and sinners in a class, forgetful of the fact that there are wide dissimilarities in each class. In a fundamental sense there are but the two classes, but in fact there are the widest diversities in each class.

Take the class sinners as including all unregenerate men. The common fact is that they all need salvation and must pass through the same experience of conviction, repentance, faith, pardon, and regeneration to obtain it; but the manner in which they are exercised will differ widely as possible. To understand this the class must be broken up and viewed in its several parts. A is a criminal of the deepest dye; B is ignorant and beastly; C has never indulged in any excesses, has been scrupulously moral; D is impulsive and excitable; E is cool and self-governing; F is intellectual and thoughtful; G has grown up amid prayers and under careful Christian nurture. It is impossible that these circumstances should not color their experiences. In one case there will be sharp and marked contrasts, in another there will be no distinctly marked change; one will enter the kingdom with a rush of feeling, another will feel but slight emotion; one will be able to point to the day and hour of his conversion, another comes into the light gradually; one is noisy and clamorous, another is quiet and silent.

It is worth while to say yet further that as there is a difference between a Christian experience and an experience of Christianity so also all of a Christian's experiences are not Christian experience. I mean this: that Christian experience is a peculiar phase of a soul's experience touching its spiritual relations which a Christian only knows any thing about; they are the specific experiences which characterize him as a Christian. But a Christian is a man, and over and above his peculiar experiences which come to him as a Christian and constitute him such—exist only as he is a Christian—he has a broad belt of experiences which come to him as a man. They are a Christian's experiences but they are also the experiences of men that are not Christians, therefore they cannot be said to be Christian experiences.

Christian defined. To determine exactly what is meant by the phrase "Christian experience" it is necessary that we define the term Christian. Though the term is one in common use, and well understood as to its general import, it is by no means explicit. There are widely variant meanings attached to it as employed by different persons even among ourselves. Popular usage falls entirely short of its strict meaning, and so becomes not only confusing but dangerously misleading; the radical idea is wholly lost, and something else, often not even suggesting it, is put in its place. Christians themselves, and not unfrequently eminently orthodox Christian teachers, fall into the snare.

Were a native of the Congo valley asked what he understands by the term he would perhaps answer, "A Christian is a man who comes in ships to barter New England rum for elephants' tusks." A Chinese would vary the definition somewhat and say: "A Christian is an outside barbarian with a white skin, who deals in opium and other foreign commodities." In fact these are prevalent definitions among these heathen peoples. There is a remote ground for the perversion. The people who carry on these nefarious practices publish themselves as Christians, and are so recognized in works of literature and history and in the popular language of the world.

If we come nearer home the term, as popularly employed, is scarcely less vague or less a perversion. Broadly, all who are born in Christian countries are called Christians: the—worse than the average heathen—rum-seller, the imbruted sot, the debauchee, the vilest creatures, men and women. So does the name cover all sin and shame.

The historian or statistician defines a Christian as one who is a citizen of a Christian state or commonwealth. Webster, our great English lexicographer, defines a Christian thus: "One who professes to believe, or is assumed to believe, in the religion of Christ: especially one whose inward and outward life is conformed to the doctrines of Christ."

If we seek the deeper significance which professed Christians attach to the term we make scarcely a nearer approach to its true meaning. An average German would probably define a Christian as one who had been baptized and confirmed in the Church of Luther; an Anglican would broaden the definition so as to include communicants of the Church of Henry the Eighth who have received the sacraments at the hands of an apostolically consecrated priest; a Romanist would exclude these, and limit the term to believers in the infallibility of Leo XIII and such as attend mass and obtain absolution; a liberal of the modern type would extend it so as to include any who practice philanthropy and have outgrown faith in a supernatural revelation or a divine Christ; others, more strict, would insist that a Christian is one who professes an orthodox creed and strictly observes the rites and ceremonies of some evangelical Church.

Recently one of the Christian weeklies sent out a request to a large number of representative writers and thinkers embracing men and women of note—ministers and laymen of all phases of faith—asking that they would return answer to the question, "What is it to be a Christian?" *

It must be admitted that the question is so phrased as to be somewhat indefinite. The object was undoubtedly to elicit an answer to the question, "What is it that constitutes a man a Christian?" The demand was strict definition. The answers in most cases show that the respondents had in mind this question rather: Who by the most liberal construction may be included in the class Christian? To this latter question strict definition was not required, but merely the setting forth of some comprehensive test characteristic. The answers, therefore, are not to be viewed as definitions, but simply general statements. But taken in this looser sense the answers are remarkable, as showing the posture of the writer's mind with regard to the deeper questions, How does a man become a Christian? and, What are the constitutive elements of his Christian character?

The definitions are all of them in one form and another beautiful and clear statements of some truth. There is not one of them that does not affirm a fact which characterizes a Christian. Most of them set forth a fact which implies the existence of every other essential fact, and so clearly points out a Christian. To be a Christian one must be what is affirmed, and being what is affirmed he will probably be a Christian. So far they designate a Christian. Seven of the thirty do not necessarily imply a Christian at all, though a Christian implies them.

Five of the thirty contain all the essential elements of true

* See note A, p. 180.

definition. Several approximate definition, and only fail by being too brief. Of all, Dr. Whedon's is the most complete.

There is apparent in most of those which approximate definition a manifest desire to broaden the definition, and a spirit of compromise which is not healthful in these times.

To determine what it is to be a Christian, that is, what is a Christian, it is necessary to take into the definition an account of how a man becomes such: what it is that makes him a Christian. He is not born a Christian. He is not a Christian by virtue of his being a man. He does not make himself a Christian. There is a process through which he passes without which he cannot be a Christian. It is what he is after the process, and at its outcome, that constitutes him a Christian. The experiences through which he passes in order to become a Christian are so essential that he cannot be a Christian without them—they are essential and necessary constituents. They must, therefore, be taken into the definition. When these subjective elementary processes are completed he has become and is a Christian, and not without or before them. They make him a Christian.

After he has become a Christian, what is it to be a Christian resolves itself into the question, How does he show himself to be a Christian? What kind of a man is he in subjective temper and objective life? What is it in these respects that differentiates him from other men? As a Christian how must he live? what principles must govern him? what must be the inner and outer facts? These inner and outer facts are essential, but they are fruits, not the constituting essence. The essential thing is the subjective life implanted in the soul. The outer expression is proof and incident, and as such *sine qua non*, but to cite them and leave the implanted life out, from which they spring as fruit, is to leave out the constituting essence. The outer form may exist as imitation merely, and instead of having a Christian we have but an imitator, paste for a diamond, possibly a sheer hypocrite without the reality. The exterior manifestation is not the reality, and it does not necessarily prove the reality—it is simply external, and may be put on. The inner subjective life is the essential thing, and when it exists the external form must exist as growth or product of the essence, and not as mere imitation—it is the necessary form which the life principle takes. Christianity is not put on, but is put in, as leaves are not put on a tree but spring from the constituting germ. As a tree without leaves would be a deformity—in fact, could not exist—so a professed Christian without the fruits of holy character would be a monstrosity—not a Christian.

There are two errors to be avoided—both equally fatal; the error of supposing one can be a Christian by clothing himself with mere objective moralities; and the no less dangerous error of assuming the possibility of subjective grace existing apart from external moralities. The subjective life is the soul, the exterior life the body. When out of a holy soul we have a holy life, we have a Christian—not otherwise; "the good tree is known by its fruits." It is the vital germ at last, however, which determines the quality both of the tree and the fruit. The essential thing is the vital germ.

It should be remembered that neither the tree nor the fruit is always or necessarily what it seems to be. We cannot, therefore, judge infallibly by appearance. Yet we must judge by appearance, with the reservation that He who searcheth the heart only knoweth what is in man, and his judgment is a righteous judgment.

It should be remembered further that, after all, and despite the wide latitude of indefiniteness attached to the term, there is and can be no indefiniteness in the fact. The term has its metes and bounds—its inclusions and exclusions. It does not embrace all. It does exclude some. We may broaden or narrow it, but it will not alter the fact.

What then is the meaning we attach to the term in the following lectures? Our answer must be in two parts. First, *negatively*: A Christian is not such by virtue of his having been born in a Christian country, or of Christian parents; or by having been baptized and confirmed in a Christian church by an apostolically consecrated priest, bishop, or pope; or by the personal acceptance or belief of the most orthodox scriptural creed; or by the strictest observance of holy rites and sacraments; or by reiterated professions of faith and of regeneration; or by the most exemplary external moralities and careful ritualistic rules of living; or by noble charities and philanthropies. These may all have more or less relative values; some of them are necessary concomitants as incidents and fruits, but they may all exist and still the essential thing be wanting.

Second, *positively*: A Christian comprehensively is a child of God by regeneration. This is the all inclusive, absolutely essential thing. It presupposes and is conditioned by certain antecedents, and does not exist without them; these are conviction of sin, repentance, faith, and forgiveness. Regeneration, which, as matter of experience, always follows or is coetaneous with these subjective states, and never precedes them or occurs without them, is the culminating fact, and is result of a direct act of God upon the soul, by which it is engrafted into Christ and becomes participant of his life, and so becomes a Christian soul. By the divine life thus imparted the forgiven soul is delivered from the guilt and bondage of sin, and has implanted in it a principle of righteousness which makes the sin which it formerly loved hateful to it; purifies its affections, desires, and motives, and strengthens its will to the obedience of the law of

God, and fills it with love to God and universal love to man. From out this soul, thus renewed with a new life, emanates if unhindered, as a fountain flows from a perennial spring, a continuous stream of virtuous and holy living. The process by which this great change is brought about is a divinely established order, and the consciousness of the soul in passing through it and living it constitutes Christian experience. To become and be a Christian one must have this conscious experience. To the virtuous and holy living, which includes all duty toward God, and toward men, and meaner things, and toward the person himself, which springs from the newly implanted life germ, should be added the inward experiences of conscious faith and trust, and holy motive and purpose, and the peace and joy which Gods give to them that love him. The total experience is that of affiliation—the consciousness of sonship.

It is not a necessity of this definition to assume that all real Christians are equally conscious of having passed through these successive stages of experience, or that they shall in every case be able clearly to discriminate these elements to themselves, much less logically state them to others. This indeed is certainly not true; but the absence of a vivid consciousness of such subjective phenomena does not necessarily imply their non-existence. With many, each special stage in the process—awakening, penitence, faith, the assurance of pardon, the inward transformation—is matter of vivid consciousness and absolute certainty: with other many, who give abundant evidence of their thorough Christian character by their fruits in temper and their practical daily life—the great inward fact of their filial relation to God—there is no such vivid consciousness. The former speak confidently, often, perhaps, overboldly, of their experience. The latter speak with trembling modesty and even hesitancy if they speak at all—they can fix no day or date when the great phenomenal change took place: they do know, however, that they love God, and their lives are redolent of grace—full of the fruits of righteousness. That in every case there has been the great subjective change, the inward transforming experience, however dimly perceived in its successive stages, there can be no rational doubt. The total outcome of the regenerate life of the soul is the same in each case of genuine Christian character.

Personal temperament, environments, habits, education, and such modifying influences, which vary so widely, furnish the explanation to a large extent of the diverse experiences among those who give full evidence of genuine Christian character: "There is a diversity of operation but one Spirit" and the same result.

It is no part of the purpose of these lectures to undertake to prove that there have been and are men in abundance who have passed through the experience here described. The testimony of millions all along through the Christian ages, from Paul the chiefest of the apostles to the most recent convert, must be relied on to establish that fact. If it fail no other evidence on that point could be of any avail.

LECTURE 2.

IMPLICATIONS AND CONDITIONING GROUNDS OF EXPERIENCE.

There are three conceivable ways of dealing with the alleged facts of Christian experience. These are—first, to deny them and resolve them into mere delusion or hypocrisies. But as the facts are facts of consciousness, attested by a vast multitude of intelligent and, by every proof, conscientious and honest witnesses, it is obvious that this ground cannot be maintained. Denial becomes mere effrontery. To make it good would require that men suppose they have consciousness which they do not have, or that the vast multitude of witnesses in the case are a set of knaves who have conspired through the ages to impose upon their fellows by declaring that they are conscious of things of which they are not conscious. This explanation may be satisfactory to minds utterly blinded by prejudice but can have no weight with candid and sensible men. Men will still believe that a fact of consciousness is knowable, and men will still believe that when a vast multitude of good men testify that they have been and are conscious of certain states of feeling they really are so conscious. As a philosophy the theory of delusion or hypocrisy is a failure—has nothing to rest upon.

The second conceivable method is to admit the facts of consciousness and explain them as the product of delusive ideas. In this theory the feelings are admitted to be real but groundless; the offspring of mere imagination—chimeras. The theory is that the mind invents or accepts the idea of God, and the idea of a law of God which he imposes on man, and the idea that man is under obligation to obey this law, and the idea that he has broken the law which he ought to have kept, and the idea that his breach of the law has made him guilty, and the idea that he is exposed to punishment, and the idea of an atonement, and the idea of repentance and faith as a condition of forgiveness. They postulate that in point of fact there are no realities answering to these ideas; but the Christian persuades himself to believe there are answering realities. Out of this belief of his springs the feeling of guilt, and the feeling of repentance, and the feeling of pardon, and all other feelings which go to make up what is called Christian experience. The feeling of guilt exists, but there is no guilt; the feeling of pardon exists, but there is no pardon; and the other feelings exist, but all of them are product of a mere belief of the mind self-invented and self-imposed. All there is in the case is a set of fancies and a set of feelings which grow out of them. These feelings are called Christian experience. This is the only theory of negation or dissent which approaches a philosophy. It is an attempt at a philosophy, and it is not without some plausible grounds, which it is due should be stated.

It is a fact that mere fancies do produce the profoundest feelings, together with the profoundest conviction of the reality of things which do not exist; as, for instance, a man passing a grave-yard in a dark night sees a white object—a bone six inches high. His imagination transforms it to a ghost. It towers up to the height of six feet; it moves and approaches him and gesticulates. He sees its waving shroud; he detects its human features; he is profoundly moved with terror. It was not a ghost; it was but a bone. His idea of it transformed it and it terrified him. Thus a fancy has power to move us.

In fact all subjective feelings are awakened by thoughts. The mental action is always first. Feeling responds to the conception in the mind. All movement in the spiritual world is from ideas; all experience subjective is born of ideas.

This fact explains the terror awakened by superstitions. Any thing supposed to be real awakens in the consciousness a corresponding feeling. Errors when accepted and believed affect the mind just as truths do. This law must be admitted. There is no possibility of rejecting it.

It is a just question, therefore, Does this fact in any way affect the validity and apologetical value of Christian experience? If so, how and to what extent? and what is the treatment required? We are compelled to answer, it does have a direct bearing and demands consideration. If the experiences can be explained as the product of delusive ideas, as any feeling may be, that being shown it takes all virtue out of Christianity and reduces it to the common level of any other superstition; that is, shows that there is nothing in it but delusion, and a delusion which springs from delusion. If the theory could be made good that the experiences are the offspring of chimeras, as it is admitted they sometimes are, the showing would destroy the system.

What, then, becomes necessary to determine the case? To this we answer, nothing is necessary as to the experiences themselves. These are admitted to be genuine. The whole matter involved turns upon the question, Are the ideas out of which the experiences emerge chimeras—mere fancies—perversions of reality? This must be determined by the mental laws by which we try and test the validity of our ideas or of the objects of our conception.

What is necessary to the theory proposed is to show that its assumption is true—that is, that there are no realities answering to the ideas out of which the conscious experiences or the subjective feelings arise. The debate turns upon the truth of these ideas. Christianity is responsible to make them good. Doubt is responsible for the showing that they are chimerical.

The ideas declared to be chimerical are these: The personality of man, the existence of God, the existence of moral law, the fact of human guilt, the experience of pardon.

It is obvious that the sponsors for this theory have set a hard task for themselves. It will take some time to work out all these points. It will require some sturdy wrestling to prove that God is a chimera. It will take still more time to convince the average man that there is no such thing as human sin while its blistering sores are felt in every soul and revoltingly visible in every hamlet. It would be interesting to see the defenders of this theory put the case to a jury, and hear the argument by which they would prove that murder and lust and incest and cruelty and the rum fiend are immaculate. But I commend to these theorists to begin the defense of their theory, not by grappling with either of the points mentioned, but with this rather: that they may get their faculties in good trim for other heavy work let them explain to us how a *molecule* got into the business of invention and how it became such an adept as to evolve in every human soul the entire ethical code. When they shall have answered this question it will be time to set them to some other tasks which their theory involves.

We cannot here enter the polemic on any of these points, as we have only days, and not years, for the discussion. It is safe to say that the advocates of the theory, when they contemplate the difficulty of the task before them, will never undertake its defense; and it is also safe to assume that the mention of the matters which the theory involves condemns it to prompt and inevitable rejection as irrational and impossible. It perishes by mere statement—without an argument. Its existence in any mind is in proof that that mind has never considered it; that it exists purely as an irrational prejudice. To call it a philosophy is to dignify stupidity with a worthy but desecrated name.

If any thing more should be necessary as a justification for dismissing this theory without argumentative refutation, it will be found in the statement and defense of the third theory. Its unfolding and rational defense contains the refutation of all competing theories.

The remaining theory is that which we defend—the Christian theory. It is based on the truth of consciousness and the honesty of those who affirm that they are conscious of certain subjective experiences. It affirms the facts. Its mode of explaining them is that they have real grounds. It adduces what these real grounds are. The grounds adduced must be adequate to account for the subjective effects developed in experience. It finds in the adequate conditioning grounds the real source of the conscious effect. A rational explanation is reached. We have thus all the requirements of a philosophy of Christian experience.

We have seen that every other theory put forward, and every other conceivable theory, fails not only to explain the facts, but also that they must be rejected on other grounds of error and falsehood. To inadequacy they add inadmissibility as irrational, and not merely as irrational but as impossible. They meet none of the requirements of a philosophy. They are mere "*bruta fulmina.*"

When there are several theories which seem equally adequate to account for phenomena, and when none of them contain inadmissible elements, the mind may be left *in dubio* as to which shall be accepted as the actual theory. But when there is but one theory which will account for the facts, and when against that theory no real objection can be urged, that theory of right demands acceptance; it, on rational principles, has right of way.

That is precisely the case we have here, which we shall now

proceed to show. The point is to show the adequate grounds of Christian experiences. For any experience there must exist certain conditioning and adequate causes. No experience is uncaused.

To put clearly before us our task we restate in brief the experience the philosophy of which we are to render. It embraces five discrete facts of consciousness: (a) Consciousness of guilt; (b) consciousness of repentance; (c) consciousness of faith; (d) consciousness of pardon and forgiveness; (e) consciousness of a new life springing in the soul; with other subsequent experiences which need not here be mentioned. The contents of these phenomena of consciousness will be more fully developed in subsequent lectures.

Our first business will be to state what are the implications of the experience. It is true that any experience furnishes its own proof and cannot be required to furnish any other; and it is also true that any experience is proof of all its necessary implications and conditioning grounds. Its existence demands their existence. The knowledge of any effect contains in it the knowledge that whatever is necessary to its existence exists. But to render a philosophy of an experience, or any effect, it is necessary to consider and understand what the conditioning implications are, and to furnish a rational vindication of them if necessary; in any event they must be vindicable. If an alleged implication is beset with insurmountable difficulties—is not rationally vindicable—the theory is driven to the expedient of alleging mystery; that is, the admission that there is no philosophy, that is, no rational explanation, of the phenomena. In such a case the mind is disturbed with uncertainty. The ground of rational certitude is taken from under it, not as to the experience, about which it is impossible it should be uncertain, but as to the alleged implications or conditioning grounds. In the presence of insurmountable difficulty as to the alleged conditioning grounds the mind is rationally shaken as to it, and is compelled to entertain the thought that possibly there is some other explanation; that is, possibly the true philosophy has not now been reached. If, on the other hand, the alleged conditioning grounds of the phenomena are adequate to explain them, and if they are rationally vindicable, and if none other can be alleged, the inevitable conviction is that we have reached the real explanation, and the mind settles down into certitude and content. It has reached the solid ground of philosophical certainty.

Now, what are the implications of Christian experience? The facts are not the implications; they are the experience. The implications are whatever is necessary to their existence—those things without which the experience could not be. What are they? Keep in mind what the experiences are, and follow us while we find their implications.

We start with the first experience named: *sense of guilt*. This is common to all souls.

Now the adequate explanation of the sense of guilt is the fact of sin; and, as we have seen, there is and can be no other explanation. The knowledge by the soul that it is guilty includes not simply a feeling of guilt, but a knowledge of the reality of that, whatever it is, which makes it feel guilty. That which creates the sense of guilt is the knowledge the soul has of the fact that it has sinned. The reality of sin no man can dispute. That which we inquire after now is what implications underlie this fact of guilt.

What is guilt? It is desert of punishment for violating a law which ought to have been obeyed, and which the violator knew and felt ought to have been obeyed. This is not a mere lexical definition of the term. It is the exact meaning which the soul itself attaches to it when it predicates guilt of itself; it is just what is in consciousness. When it says I am guilty it means to affirm I have broken a law which I knew I ought to have kept, and my consciousness is that I am condemned—I feel it, I know it. Every soul knows perfectly what it means by having precisely that experience.

My first point is that the experience of guilt is conditioned on the spiritual nature of man.

Guilt is spiritualistic. It demonstrates the spiritual world. If there were no other fact it, standing alone, necessitates that its subject should be a self-conscious, intelligent, free, responsible spirit. It is impossible to predicate guilt of a thing under the law of necessitation. Let any one undertake to conceive of a being or thing that has no intelligence, no self-consciousness, that knows nothing, being guilty and feeling guilty, he will immediately discover that it is impossible for him to think it; or let him conceive of a being that is driven by necessity, that has no power in itself to determine its states and acts, that it is what it is by imposed constitution, and does what it does with no power to the alternative, he will find no difficulty to think such a being, but he will find it impossible to attach the idea of guilt to it; for that he must find another kind of subject: an intelligent and self-determining being and one who has the idea and feeling of oughtness, or obligation to a definite course of action. If the molecular universe is under the law of necessity, which is the last and unquestioned deliverance of science, the very norm of science, the molecular universe excludes guilt. In that realm it cannot be found—it cannot even be thought as possible. Its presence proclaims a non-molecular, that is, a spiritual, subject. The same result follows from all other phenomena of Christian experience: repentance, faith, pardon, regeneration, adoption. These predicates require as conditioning ground a spiritual being. Try to think of a molecular being, a being composed of material atoms, a compound of "carbonic acid, water, and ammonia"—Huxley's definition of man—organized and driven by necessity, assuming to itself to be an ego, and then predicating of itself I am guilty, and, on the ground of guilt for being what it is by necessity, repenting, exercising faith, and supplicating pardon, and then receiving pardon from the being who made it what it is; and it will at once be discovered how utterly absurd and ridiculous the thing is. Nothing is plainer than that guilt and pardon, and all their attendant and concomitant experiences, require a spiritual subject, under law but free as to its action, and possessing alternative power. Christian philosophy is responsible for this underlying, conditioning postulate. It rests upon it. If it can be shaken the ground of both guilt and pardon will be removed. Disprove the spirituality of man, the whole theory topples into chaos. The phenomena of feeling would, however, remain to be explained. With the spirituality of man as conditioning ground the phenomena are perfectly intelligible. Without it reason becomes confounded, and is compelled to admit that it has no explanation to offer.

While a non-free being cannot be guilty by possibility, it is obvious that a being who knows his law, and has power to obey it, and feels the obligation to obey it, cannot but be guilty if he violates it, and only a free being can violate its law. Guilt demonstrates, and does not merely render probable, the personality of man; that is, that he is an intelligent and free spirit. There is no explanation possible of the fact without the implication.

I have said that guilt is spiritualistic; that there can be no guilt without a free personal subject; but I now say there can be a free personal subject without guilt. Guilt necessitates a personal subject, but a personal subject does not necessitate guilt. There are, we may safely believe, millions of personal subjects who know nothing of guilt. But there is not one being who can feel guilt and not be a free spirit.

The idea of pardon becomes absurd in the absence of conscious freedom on the part of the subject of pardon. Pardon for what? For being or doing what it was impossible to the subject to avoid? Pardon by whom? By the being who necessitated the action? Both guilt, which involves personal fault, and pardon, which implies penalty, are fatal to any system of materialistic necessity; and no less so to any system of necessitating agency of God in respect to acts or states which are assumed to involve guilt. Pardon to an unfree being is as absurd as pardon to a material substance for being influenced by the law of gravitation or any other law. Right and wrong, as ethical terms, are meaningless as applied to any unfree act or state; whether in the spiritual or material universe. The sense of right and wrong to an unfree being is impossible. The sense of obligation to one act or state as against another act or state to an unfree being is a delusion and a snare. The entire ethical system perishes under the idea of necessity. Thus fundamental to all ethical experiences, such as sense of obligation to any given thing, feeling of guilt for any given thing, repentance for any given thing, or pardon for any given thing, is the idea of freedom in the case.

My second point is that Christian experience requires a personal God, and is conditioned upon that ground.

Guilt is also theistic. There can be no guilt without God. If it requires a free subject it also requires a binding law. There can be no guilt without a law which imposes obligation on the subject, but which at the same time does not necessitate him. But a law which imposes obligation to obedience must be authoritative, and must be felt to be so; otherwise neither the idea nor sense nor fact of obligation could be felt; and without these, and not simply without these ideas but also without the absolute fact of obligatoriness, it is impossible that guilt should exist. But a law to be obligatory and authoritative must be instituted and enforced by a being who has the right and also the power to enact and enforce it. Without such a being there can be no law and no guilt. Guilt, therefore, has as necessary condition precedent God. Allow the fact of guilt, it is impossible to disallow the fact of God. The possibility of the one necessitates the actuality of the other. In the last result guilt involves, that is, it is of its essence, that there is an oughtness and an oughtnotness; and these ideas have no standing-ground outside of God. The ethic is in him and of him. Take him away, the entire ethical system perishes. But if now we pass beyond the experience of guilt to the experience of pardon we find as an implication or conditioning ground of this further experience not simply the idea and fact of God, as Author and Administrator of law, enforcing obligation; we do still find this, but we find additionally a being who has the right and the power to cancel guilt, and one who exercises that power and right. For this implication Christian philosophy is responsible; that is, it must be able to render a rational account of it. It demands that there is a being who is above all law except the law he finds in his own nature, and who has the right and obligation to his own nature to enact and administer laws over all other beings.

There is theism without guilt. Heaven is theistic; holiness is theistic; all angels are theists. There can be a God in a universe in which no guilt is, but there can be no guilt in a universe where no God is. Guilt is proof of a God.

Pardon implies five things: (*a*) that there is nothing in the nature of guilt that renders it absolutely irremissible under all circumstances: if it were, pardon would forever be impossible; (*b*) that there is nothing in the nature of God or in his administrative relations to the universe that renders pardon absolutely impossible to him, otherwise guilt would be absolutely irremissible and pardon could not exist; (*c*) that in order to terminate guilt there must be an administrative act of pardon: it cannot terminate itself; (*d*) that there is a disposition on the part of God to exercise the pardoning power; (*e*) that there is nothing in the circumstances of guilt, or in the nature of God, or in his administrative relations to the universe, which absolutely demands that he should in any case exercise the pardoning power unconditionally.

These principles we regard as of fundamental importance, but time will not permit us to enter upon the polemic which would be demanded for their support. One of the five, however, we feel called upon to note more at length; namely, that the fact of pardon implies not simply the power and right to pardon, but also a disposition to do so. If God were not disposed to pardon it is impossible there should be any pardon, since it is impossible to conceive of his doing any thing to which he is absolutely indisposed. But if the exercise of the pardoning power depended solely on his disposition to pardon it would require that it should be exercised in every case. There could then be no distinction between righteousness and unrighteousness in his administration. The ethical system would be plunged into chaos. The disposition to pardon must, therefore, find a limit to its exercise both in his nature and in the general welfare of the universe. Thus we find that with the disposition to pardon revealed in the fact of pardon, there must be conditions on which he will exercise the power. The disposition is not a disposition to pardon indiscriminately, universally, or on the principle of arbitrary selection, or in any case unconditionally. He will pardon when the interests of righteousness, that is, of right administration, will permit it.

The experience requires as a conditioning ground not simply a personal God, but an infinitely holy God. It requires that his holiness should not be simply the holiness of immaculate purity that cannot tolerate moral impurity—it does require that —but also the holiness of infinite and eternal love, that must include in it compassion for the sinful, and that must in all possible ways seek to save any who may have sinned; *in all possible ways*, which means ways possible to the ethical nature of God and the ethical nature of sinning creatures.

My third point is, Christian experience is Christic; that is, *it requires Christ as a conditioning ground.* That this is so theologically and scripturally is not what is meant. That would resolve itself into a mere question of what the Bible teaches. But that is not the matter we have in hand. We are not at present set to find what the Bible teaches. That were comparatively an easy task. It is ours—a much more difficult task—to find the philosophy of our experience.

And the point we now make is that the experience itself cannot be explained without Christ, and is explained with Christ. No Christ, no Christian experience; or no possible explanation of the experience.

The experience to which we now particularly call attention is that of pardon. The existence of the race as guilty and needing pardon is condition precedent to pardon, and in a future discussion it will appear that that fact requires Christ as its explanation.

The guilty race has its existence in him, and could not exist without him, on fundamental ethical grounds, and not on mere scriptural grounds; but that is not the point we at present seek to develop.

The point we now make is that the experience of pardon implicates Christ, and cannot be explained without him. We have already shown that pardon, which is an administrative act of God, implies a disposition on his part to pardon; but we have also shown that the disposition could not result in unconditional pardon, since that would subvert the ethical system. Pardon, if administered, must be on conditions which would preserve the holiness of the administration. Christ furnishes that condition in his atoning work, and this appears in the experience. The experience is not simply pardon, but pardon conditioned by atonement in Christ. It is not pardon without Christ, but pardon through Christ. This is not simply the teaching of the Scriptures, but it is the experience.

The Christian experience is that pardon is received on two conditioning grounds—repentance toward God and faith in Jesus Christ. When this repentance is adequate and faith is exercised, the soul becomes conscious of pardon, and not until that. The faith is faith in Christ as an atoning Saviour.

Now this fact of the administration proves one of two things: either that the pardoning act is based upon a pure fiction and a faith which is utterly false, or that there is a real atoning Christ who conditions the pardon. If we take the former view it will require that God conditions pardon upon a fiction, and that in order to it he requires or honors, as condition precedent, faith in a pure fable, and bases his administration upon a falsehood. To escape this atonement in Christ must be real, and so the requirement of faith be vindicable on principles of truth and righteousness.

How atonement becomes available to pardon is a point to be considered further on. That which we now affirm is that Christ is a necessary conditioning ground to the experience of pardon under the Christian dispensation: so necessary that it cannot be explained without him. I cannot here enter the polemic as to the person of Christ—the question of his divinity—a question having important relations to the philosophy of pardon. What I do affirm is that the experience of pardon on faith in Christ requires a *de facto* Christ, and the *de facto* Christ embraced in the faith—Christ an Atoner, through whom the pardon is administered.

It is Christic, since it cannot exist where Christ is not known, and since it cannot exist where Christ is known, except by faith in him, and since it invariably exists where faith is exercised in him. It is impossible to explain it without Christ.

I have said that Christian experience is Christic. There may be Christ and an atonement and possibly no Christian experience, but there can be no Christian experience without Christ and his atonement. The experience is proof positive of Christ and of atonement in Christ.

My fourth point is: Christian experience requires as its conditioning ground the office and work of an omnipresent agent, the Holy Ghost. That this is a scriptural doctrine no one acquainted with the teaching of the sacred books will call in question. But this is not what I am set to ascertain and defend. My work is to show that the experience demands it.

What is the particular experience to be accounted for which requires the action of any other personal agent in the soul than the soul itself? The phenomena to be accounted for are: Sense of guilt, contrition of heart, the commitment of the soul to God, consciousness of pardon, the *radical revolution of the soul in its affections, and entire volitional* life, and a consciousness of the divine favor. These comprise the elements of the experience.

To account for these experiences, we must attribute them to the soul itself as product of its own action pure and simple; or we must find them as product of some other agent inworking them by its sole efficiency; or we must find them as product of the coaction of the soul with another agent operating with it and in it.

Sin is an act, or both an act and state, of the soul. Consciousness of the act or state of sin might conceivably account for the deep conviction of guilt without supposing any other coacting agent. But I am safe in affirming that it accords with the experience that the soul is not alone in the experience. In conviction there is the consciousness of another with the soul. We think there can be no mistake about this. That consciousness must be explained. Repentance is also an act and state of the soul. It is conceivable that the soul is sufficient alone to account for it; but here again we think there can be no mistake that there is the consciousness of a supernatural presence with the soul in its struggles for pardon. Men are not alone either in their conviction of sin or their repentance, or in their final act of faith. There is throughout the conscious coaction of another with the soul—helping, encouraging, inspiring. No one who has passed through the experience will doubt this.

In the yet deeper experience of forgiveness the consciousness is of a witnessing to that fact by the pardoner. Of this there is concurrent testimony, not by all who give good evidence of Christian character, but by a large proportion of such. This consciousness is to be accounted for. The natural explanation is that the pardoner attests his own act. Allowing that a *de facto* pardon has taken place, it is inconceivable that the pardoner should not witness to it—that he should leave the soul to the hazard of mere inference. As a fact he is present, for he is the Omnipresent.

But, if now we pass to the still deeper experience of the new life which springs in the soul, this must be accounted for. However there may be obscurity as to the fact of the direct witnessing of God to the forgiveness act, there is no uncertainty as to the springing of a new life in the forgiven soul. There is no fact of consciousness more explicit than this. The revolution is complete and radical. The soul knows it as it knows itself. The affections change their objects. What was loved is now hated; what was hated is now loved. The motives which were dominant are displaced, and new motives emerge. The masters once regnant are driven out and a new king is enthroned. The whole current of the life is changed, and this often in a moment. The will, once rebellious, is now loyal. "Old things have passed away, all things have become new"—the man is born again.

These facts, for they are facts, demand an adequate explanation. If the facts referred to mere externalities—mere change of conduct or the adoption of new principles, new governing ideas, there might be no need to go beyond the soul itself for the explanation. However difficult that task, a strong will, sustained by a clear conviction, might be adequate to it. It has often occurred with no other cause than self-determination. But that is not the case we have here to be accounted for. The case we offer is totally different. It is the case of a soul *subjectively* changed—a soul revolutionized. To this, we affirm, the soul itself has no power. The will has no power over either the affections or motives. It can go adverse to them, but it cannot change them. The soul cannot *righteous* (Bushnell) itself. The sources of this change must be from above or from without. The soul must be a co-factor in the change; it cannot take place without it, but it must have the concurrence and co-working of a power superior to itself. To effect this great change, like passing from death unto life—in the fact, a change from death unto life—it requires that its guilt should be purged by forgiveness; a guilty soul cannot be a righteous soul, and it requires that it should be in the fellowship of the divine life—that the fountain should be opened in it. This great change demands God with and in the soul both as forgiving and renewing.

The soul has no power to revolutionize itself. It has power to determine its volitional activity within certain limits. It can determine to break off from sin, but it cannot purge itself of sin. It can determine to seek forgiveness, but it cannot forgive itself. It can, with divine help, commit itself to God, and, in a word, do all that is required of it in order to its salvation, but it has no power to save itself. God only can save; God only can put his life into the soul; God only can revolutionize the affections and transform the soul from the love of sin to the love of holiness. This act of new creation is not required of the soul itself simply because it is out of its power. God requires of it that it shall furnish the conditions within its power, on which he can effect the great change in it from spiritual death to spiritual life.

If the facts of Christian experience are conditioned upon certain preconceptions, or more yet upon certain ground facts, in such manner that the phenomena cannot be explained or their existence rationally conceived without the reality of the conditioning facts, then the phenomena become demonstration of the reality of the conditioning grounds, just as any phenomena point to the reality of that which gives rise to them or of which they are phenomena. Thought, self-consciousness, rational volition, demand a personal subject; and where the phenomena are found mind must exist as conditioning ground or cause. Form, color, gravity demand matter and cannot be explained without it. The phenomena, wherever found, proclaim the conditioning ground. In like manner, the consciousness of sin, which is but another name for the consciousness—that is, the knowledge—of the transgression of law, demands the existence of a law that is transgressed. The phenomena of consciousness demonstrate the existence of the law. If the consciousness is that the law is imposed and binding, and not a self-created imagination, the phenomena point to and demonstrate an objective source—the law demonstrates a lawgiver just as certainly as guilt demonstrates a law-breaker. So, further, if the breaking of the law involves guilt—that is, liability to punishment and personal demerit—the guilt incurred by the violation of law demonstrates the freedom of the violator, since guilt cannot attach to any necessitated act. Thus the fact of human sin, attended with the phenomenon of conscious guilt, demonstrates the existence of God as lawgiver, the personality and responsibility of man as a free personal being, and the entire substance of an ethical system.

If, further, among the phenomena of Christian experience there emerges the consciousness of pardon this phenomenon proclaims a pardoning power in the administration of the moral system who has authority to suspend or restrain the penalties affixed to violations of law. If the pardon is consciously obtained through or at the end of repentance and faith as conditioning ground, and if the faith required and exercised is faith in Jesus Christ as an Atoner and Saviour in some way and for some cause, then the pardon, consciously experienced, can only be explained by the reality of Christ and his redeeming act. It arises solely on this ground. The experience is moral demonstration of the reality of the conditioning cause of the phenomena of pardon and forgiveness. If pardon is attended with a life implanted or a conscious renovation or regeneration of the soul receiving the pardon, the accompanying regeneration demands the regenerating agent just as much as any effect demands its appropriate cause. All effects are signs—phenomena of causes.

I name as final conditioning fact to Christian experience the truth and knowledge of revelation. There is, and can be, no Christian experience outside of the knowledge of the Bible and the knowledge communicated in the Bible. This I affirm is a fact. The fact shows that the Bible is a necessary conditioning ground to the experience.

Upon the announcement of this postulate the question immediately springs in your minds, What of the heathen, and what of infants, and what of the multitude of souls who cannot be said to have any proper knowledge of any spiritual truth? To this question I answer, it is certain that neither a heathen who has never heard of Christ, nor an infant who as yet knows nothing, nor an immature or imbecile intellect that has no ethical possibilities, can be a Christian or have all the elements of Christian experience. They all lack the necessary conditions of Christian experience, which, in sum, is the knowledge of God as he has revealed himself to men in his holy word and in Jesus Christ, his Son. That is a fact which cannot be disputed.

My thesis does not require me to deal further with the question, but simply to point out the grounds of Christian experience and furnish a rational explanation of it. I might pass on without giving further attention to the side question which springs in your minds, but you would not be satisfied with that, I am sure.

What of the heathen? what of infants? what of imbeciles? I have said they cannot be Christians. Does any body doubt it? But must they then be lost? Why should they be lost? For not being what it is impossible they should be, and that by no fault of their own? Did God ever require an impossibility? Who will dare to say so? Did he ever condemn a soul for not being or not doing what it was forever impossible, without fault of its own, it should be or do? Who dares to say it? There is a great temptation to branch off into a theological discussion, but I must demonstrate my theory of the will by resisting the temptation. The subject is fully discussed in *Studies in Theology*.

I think it must appear to all, to say the least, a very remarkable fact that the phenomena which emerge in Christian experience demand precisely those conditioning grounds which have been cited, and which are laid down in the Scriptures and cannot be explained without them. When a theory is propounded on a given subject, the scientific norm for determining the truth of the theory is that the theory accounts for all the facts. When it does this, and the facts cannot be accounted for in any other way, the theory itself is considered as rationally established. This is precisely the case we have here. The facts to be accounted for are of the class of facts best known— the facts of consciousness—facts of experience. The specific facts are, a human soul conscious of guilt, a human soul conscious of repentance, a human soul conscious of pardon, a human soul conscious of a radical change in its loves, aspirations, motives, emotions, purposes, all its subjective ethical feelings and permanent states; as to all these a new creature. The conditioning grounds alleged as explanatory of the facts or phenomena are the soul, a free responsible being, a law broken, a sovereign Lawgiver, a Redeemer, through whom pardon is extended, a renewing Holy Spirit by whom the soul is regenerated. These conditioning grounds adequately account for the phenomena, and there is no other possible way of accounting for them; and so the phenomena point to and demonstrate the reality of the conditioning grounds.

It is in noticeable harmony with this that those who deny any one of these fundamenta to Christian experience, say the personality of the human soul, or the personality of God, or the historical verity of Jesus Christ and his redemptive work, or the personality and office of the Holy Spirit, one or all, are sure also to deny the reality of Christian experience and resolve the whole series of phenomena into sheer delusion or absolute hypocrisy; and, contrariwise, those who make small account of Christian experience are certain to be skeptical on one or all of these fundamenta. The two interests are so inseparably interblended that one invariably and by logical necessity carries the other. The essence of Christianity requires both and perishes in the absence of either.

The statement here made does not render it necessary to affirm that among sects which theoretically deny some of these fundamenta, say, the redemptive work of Christ, or the proper Godhood of Christ, or the office and work of the Holy Spirit as a distinct personality, or the implied doctrine of the Trinity, there are no Christians. Such an affirmation would be uncharitable and without support of evidence. Without doubt there is a spiritual instinct, a faith of the heart, that many times goes deeper than a creed, and not unfrequently adverse to it. It is not for us either to judge or dogmatically affirm as to what may be the possibilities of grace under the embarrassments of a defective creed; nor, further, is it necessary to deny that an experience of saving grace equivalent to a Christian experience as ground of peace and ultimate salvation may be attained even by a heathen soul who never heard of Christ or the Holy Ghost.

What we do affirm is that the fundamenta named are indispensable *conditions* of *Christian* experience and of all saving experience, whether they are recognized or not. That the clear apprehension of them is important to a clear experience cannot be reasonably doubted. That intellectual confusion with regard to any one of them tends to obscure all spiritual consciousness of grace we are compelled to believe; but that a *de facto* redemption may be made available by the Holy Spirit, whose office and even whose existence is dogmatically denied, grace triumphing over defects of intellectual apprehension, we also do not find it possible to doubt. Hindered by mental obscuration, the soul may, and probably, I think I may say certainly, often does, find its way to the all-loving Saviour imperfectly conceived of.

We hold as axiomatic that any sincere and earnest soul, under any dispensation or in any possible outward darkness, honestly and according to its best light seeking God, will find its way to him, and by means of a redemption wrought by Christ, even if it have no knowledge of it or him, will, by the ever-present Holy Spirit, come to salvation; but though a soul so circumstanced may be saved through Christ, it cannot, by reason of its circumstances, have a Christian experience, but only the essential equivalent of it. No other view can be held without consigning to inevitable destruction the entire heathen world, which in all the ages past and at present comprises almost the entire mass of mankind. Of the exact processes of the Holy Spirit in regenerating the heathen, and also in regenerating infants, nothing is revealed and nothing can be known. To doubt that there is a process is to impeach the administration of Jehovah with diabolical cruelty and injustice.

LECTURE 3.

ANTECEDENT HISTORY AND PRINCIPLES WHICH COLOR EXPERIENCE.

The universe is a free product of God. To say that he had a purpose in its creation is only to say that he is an intelligent being and acts as such. To say that that purpose was the highest possible is only to say that he is the infinitely wise and good. That purpose must have had respect both to himself and to the universe to be. For himself it could have been no less a purpose than his own highest glory—that is, that the total outcome should most perfectly accord with his infinite perfections, should most perfectly manifest them, and should so serve his own highest blessedness of perfect self-content. It is impossible to conceive that he should have proposed any thing less than this for himself without ascribing to him moral defect of some kind. For the universe itself his purpose must have been that it should be so planned and made as to attain in the total outcome the highest good that could possibly be secured to created existence, for to aim at any thing less than this would imply moral defect—that is, defect in goodness. If infinite wisdom could have devised any thing better than that which was devised, and if infinite power could have caused it to be, infinite goodness must have purposed it, unless we suppose that infinite goodness could prefer and did prefer that which is not best to that which is best, which is a contradiction. The result is that the universe that is comprehending the total outcome is the best *possible* to its maker, most perfectly manifesting his glory, and to the greatest possible degree securing his blessedness, and at the same time having secured to it the greatest good possible to infinite wisdom, power, and goodness. All of which is but saying that a person possessed of perfect wisdom, perfect power, and perfect goodness, and acting out these attributes, must choose and execute the best thing possible.

Any system made to serve the ends of infinite wisdom and goodness must be regulated by law. Lawlessness is chaos. The universe exists, therefore, under law. The source of law is not only by right but of necessity the author of the system. The system includes its laws and does not exist apart from them.

In the natural system the will of the author is law and conformity is enforced by his power. In the ethical system his will is law enjoined upon the subject but conformity is not enforced, but left at the option of the subject, with amenability.

Under the natural system the quality of the thing made is concrete—posited in its creation; that is, it serves just the end it was created to serve. In the ethical system the subject is created with powers inherent, but his ethical quality is self-determined by the use he makes of his power. Voluntary, unenforced conformity or disconformity to his law determines his quality. His quality is not concreated but is self-produced. Under the ethical system there must be a period and opportunity during which the subject shall furnish the proof what his volitional course and disposition will be with respect to his law—that is, what manner of being he will determine himself to be. This period is called probation. There is no place for probation in the natural system; it is a necessity in the ethical system.

Under probation the subject determines his quality, and there is no other way in which it could be determined. It cannot be concreated; it must be self-originated. It may be to infinite wisdom foreknown.

When the quality of the subject has been *finally* self-determined by his volitional conformity or disconformity to the law enjoined upon him, it is a real quality of righteousness or unrighteousness, as the case may be, and will at the end of probation be irreversible—that is, such that he will not reverse it. The quality thus self-superinduced must determine how the subject shall be disposed of under law. There is an immutable ethical necessity that he should be disposed of according to his character of righteous or unrighteous.

Man is a spirit, and as such he comes under the law of the spiritual world and not under the law of things. Christian experience is of the Spirit and is purely spiritual. It is to be interpreted wholly from this stand-point.

Now, what is the law of the spiritual as contradistinguished from the law in the natural world? In the natural world the reigning law is that of necessity—all effects are necessitated effects. One all-embracing and comprehensive power explains every thing. All events are forced and directed by one sovereign will. It is pure monergism. Were this the only constitution the universe would be reduced to mere things driven by necessitating force. Under such a system it would be impossible to introduce or locate the idea of responsibility anywhere below the necessitating agent. Upon such a foundation it would be impossible for an ethical system to arise. Pure monergism excludes ethics. Nature knows no ethics. Throughout all its realm the word ought finds no place, and that simply because of its reigning law. The law of the spiritual world is fundamentally different. Spirits are free, self-determining beings. They are not driven by necessity either from within or without. The sources of their action are subjective—that is, self-inhering. The constitution under which they exist is that of free personal powers. Any interpretation of them and their expression must recognize this fundamental law; but though free powers they are not without laws for their government.

As they are different in constitution from things, they being self-determining powers, and things being not powers at all, but mere concrete expressions of a power by which they exist, so they are different in governing laws, the laws of things being simply the rules of action of the being who constitutes them and drives them, and the laws of free spirits being rules of action enjoined upon them by their creator for their government, but to the obedience of which they are free—that is, not necessitated—but are held responsible; that is, are under obligation of duty and are answerable for delinquency.

The spiritual world exists and is administered under this fundamental constitution over all realms where it is found for ever and ever. It is the fundamentum of an ethical system. Any experiences in the spiritual world are to be interpreted by it.

Of the spiritual world our knowledge is limited, but there is, and necessarily must be, one reigning constitution throughout. Under that constitution it is certain that every responsible spirit has to undergo some kind of a probation upon the outcome of which its ultimate destiny depends. There are and can be no untested responsible spirits in the universe. Probation is a necessary inclusion of any ethical system administered over fallible beings. As it is a necessity to a moral being that he should be free to his law, so it is a necessity that it should be possible for him to break his law and come under its condemnation. Probation simply means a period, long or short, during which there shall be a fair and adequate opportunity furnished to establish the fact whether a free being will permanently respect the obligations of duty, and at the end of which, having had a fair trial, he shall be answerable for his conduct. The implications of a probation which shall terminate in a fixed ethical character, and ultimate ethical state of reward or penalty, are not simply that the trial shall have been beneficently fair, but that during the trial the subject shall have assumed an attitude to obligatory law which to it is of its own choice final. Until that stage is reached it is impossible that probation should terminate, under a beneficent system.

The exact circumstances under which other spirits not of the human race have undergone their probation are unknown to us. There is room for great possible diversity. We will not enter the field of conjecture.

What is probation? It will aid to the right understanding of the case if we give yet more specific attention to what is involved in the idea of probation. The term itself means to try or test; a method of trying and testing. When applied to a person it means that he is subjected to tests to determine his ethical quality, that is, that he may furnish the proof of what manner of person he is, and will permanently be. But the object of probation is not simply to determine the quality of the person tested, but that, the quality being determined, a basis may be furnished for the proper disposition of the person tested. In the case of man, or any spirit, the end of the testing or probation is that he may furnish the proof of his ethical quality, and so be assigned his permanent proper place under ethical law.

Now there are several implications in this which need to be noted and which must determine the righteousness of the proceeding.

I note then, first, in order to an ethical probation the ethical idea must exist in the probationer; that is, there must be the idea of right and wrong, and there must be felt obligation to the right. In a universe where these correlate ideas did not exist there could be no ethical character, and so no ethical tests.

I note, second, the subject must be put under law which enjoins the right, and creates in the subject the feeling of obligation to it, which necessitates that the subject should know the law, and should feel not only obliged to it but obliged by it, because it enjoins what the subject believes to be right. The ethical quality of the act of obedience demands not only that the law should be kept, but that it should be kept because the subject believes that it ought to be kept. It is this sense of oughtness which puts ethical quality in the act of obedience, not simple obedience itself.

I note, third, that in order to ethical probation the subject must not only know his law and feel under obligation to obey it, but he must be fully able to obey it, and at the same time must have power to disobey it. For if he have no power to obey it it is impossible that he should be under obligation to obey it, and it is also impossible that failure to obey should be any test of his ethical quality; and, contrariwise, if he have no power to disobey it obedience is no ethical test. It follows that the subject, while obliged by the requirement of the law, cannot be necessitated by internal or external force. He must feel the obligation of duty or oughtness, but must be free from constraint. It is this which lifts him into ethical quality, and distinguishes him from mere things.

I note, fourth, that not only must the subject be free, so that the act may be his own proper personal act and so determine his ethical quality, but it must, in order to be a real test, be an act not simply to which he is free with alternative power to the opposite, but it must be an act in the presence of such influences to the opposite as furnish the proof that his adherence to the right is such that under no possible exigencies of his existence it will ever be reversed. The test is a final test, and furnishes to infinite wisdom the conditions of a final disposition of the case, so that the probation ends and destiny is reached.

It thus appears that under any ethical system the evil of disconformity to its law must be possible to the subject, and the evil of punishment be a necessity when such disconformity exists by final choice.

Whether a soul can be saved without probation, that is, forever fixed in happiness without having passed through a probation, is a point about which it is impossible to know, but it is absolutely certain that no soul can be condemned or consigned to inevitable curse without an equitable probation. If heaven may be given as a free gift without conditions, and if one may be perpetually holy without ever having passed through the hazards of the opportunity and temptation to choose evil, it is absolutely an impossible idea, on ethical grounds, that any one should be consigned to hell without opportunity of an opposite fate, and impossible also that he should enjoy heaven without a choice of holiness. How God saves infants and imbeciles is not revealed, but that it is impossible they should be lost is one of the clearest ethical certainties; and that it is impossible they should be saved without a free adherence to righteousness is equally certain—holiness is self-determined and *vice versâ*, and holiness constitutes heaven. The case of the heathen is that they are amenable to the law under which they exist, and under it serve their probation.

To man there is but one probation, and that it is in time and while he is in the body we believe on scriptural grounds, and on no other. We do not therefore undertake to give a philosophy of it. We do see that a perfectly equitable probation in which there is an adequate and fair opportunity to a happy issue in every case is an ethical necessity. The method and time-limit of probation, revealed or not, is one which infinite wisdom and goodness will devise, and which will approve itself to the universe as both just and generous. No human soul, infantile, imbecile, or heathen, exists or will be disposed of for eternity apart from atonement in Christ, and no soul can fail of the benefits of the atonement unto eternal salvation without personal incorrigible sin against the light vouchsafed. These are points determined by immutable ethical principles.

The circumstances under which a human soul passes its probation are important to be noted, as they furnish an explanation of its peculiar experiences. There can be no philosophy of Christian experience without taking account of them. The statement will have to be somewhat extended, but will be reduced to as brief limits as possible.

The first point we note as having bearing is this, human souls have a racial origin—they, while having an individualized identity, which separates each soul from every other soul so as to make it a distinct being, do not severally exist alone and apart, but come into existence in a race order and derive something affecting their state from heredity. We cannot here introduce the polemic on traducianism and creationism.

The second point we note is, every human soul propagated in fact enters upon its existence and upon its probation in an abnormal condition, that is, in inherent disconformity with its law—a state propagated in it. This fact tinges its whole experience as a soul, and gives rise to all the peculiar phenomena of Christian experience.

We might pass on without further consideration of this point, but the result would be unsatisfactory. The question how abnormalcy came to be a fact becomes important as affecting points which will emerge further on, and needs a brief treatment.

To answer this question we need to push our researches further back, into earlier incidents of our race history.

The next point I note, therefore, is, that the head of our race was a *created* soul who was placed on his probation in a normal state. I do not enter upon the polemic here as to the measure of either his intellectual or moral or spiritual endowments. The only point I make is he had nothing intrinsic, and there was nothing extrinsic in disharmony with his law. The law under which he was placed was suited to his capacity, and there was nothing abnormal in him or in his environments to hinder or embarrass a fair probation; there was every thing in both respects to aid to a desirable outcome.

The next point I note is this, to which I attach the greatest possible emphasis; his probation was for himself alone. It seems strange that it should be necessary to emphasize this point, since it is in contradiction of fundamental ethics that it should have been otherwise. The only excuse for the emphasis is that a vicious theologizing, running through the centuries, has assiduously taught that he served a probation for his unborn posterity.

The next point I note is, that this first created soul failed in his probation; that is, he broke the law given him, and never given to any one of his posterity, and became liable to its penalty, which was declared to be death. The occasion of the failure was temptation. The sources of the temptation were external and internal. He was tempted by a malign spirit. He was also prompted by his own constitution. There was food for temptation stored in him. The law suggested resistance, because it forbade something the soul desired. It is so in every moral act.

It is important to note the difference between temptation and sin, and also the difference between temptableness and sinfulness. Temptation is not sin. There can be no sin without temptation; and also there can be no probation and no ethical subject without temptation or temptableness. Temptation is felt solicitation to sin, with a conscious ability to comply with the solicitation and an attraction to it. Sin is the yielding of the will to the solicitation under the sense of obligation to the opposite, and with power to the opposite. The solicitation to sin does not mar the moral integrity of the tempted soul, nor does the feeling of its attraction. It taxes its will and puts it under stress. When the temptation is resisted it strengthens the will and tends to establish the soul in righteousness. By a series of resistances of solicitation to sin solicitation loses its power, and there comes a time when the influence of temptation diminishes to zero, and the will strengthened by exercise, or the soul, will forever stand in the perfect and immovable integrity of righteousness. When that point is reached probation has answered its end and destiny is determined—the soul is forever sphered in holiness and the perfect rest and peace of eternal life. So, contrariwise, when the will yields itself to the solicitation of sin it sins. It is the yielding that is the sin. With the yielding temptation acquires additional power, and the power to resist is weakened. Ultimately the power to resist is reduced to zero, and the influence of evil is raised to complete dominance. Character is fixed in irreversible sin, that is, the soul has freely determined itself to sin by a free choice which under no circumstances in its future history it will reverse. Probation ends and destiny begins—the soul is lost.

It may be of advantage to note the avenue of temptation to the unfallen Adam. Doubtless the sources of temptation are varied, as the environing circumstances of individual spirits vary. The temptations by which angels lost their first state are not revealed, and there is nothing in common between their plane and ours by which we can interpret them.

The case of Adam is stated and it is perfectly intelligible to us. His temptation arose through the sensuous and intellectual nature he possessed. His law—a divine statute, not a constitutional law—forbade him to partake of a certain fruit. The law became the occasion of temptation. He desired that which was forbidden for two reasons; it appealed to his sensuous nature, it appealed also to his intellectual nature. It attracted him because it looked as if it would be pleasant to taste. It attracted him because it would broaden his knowledge. He was so made that these two facts could not fail to create desire. The desire became source of temptation. Note, there was no sin in the desire. That was natural, and with his constitution was inevitable. It was that fact that made the law a test. If the forbidden object had not been adapted to awaken desire there would have been no probation or no test in the case. His sin commenced not with desire, but with the going over of the will to the choice of the forbidden thing. All sin has its seat in the will. The appetites and passions and intellectual aspirations are not sins. They belong to the original furnishings of the soul. Sin is volitional indulgence in contravention of law. So long as the desires are kept within bounds of law they are proper and right, serve a constitutional function, and accord with the will of God. They are limited by law. When the will which is appointed to govern them and keep them within law, turns traitor to its trust sin is the result.

Let us try to get as nearly as possible at the exact truth

aimed at by all these and similar statements. To do this, we begin with the statement that man is a being who has relations to a sensuous and supersensuous world. He was made for final existence in the supersensuous realm. That was to be his home, and in its employments he was to find his perfected bliss. His faculties were to be awake and opened to its realities, and his supreme affections to be set on it. The thought of it was to be the supreme power molding his life and pursuits. He was to live in expectancy of it and under its abiding influence. Supreme love to God and absolute subjection of himself to God was to be the governing norm of his life. But he was also placed in an animal body, which related him temporarily to a sensuous world which appealed to him in various ways, and had power with him in various inferior ministries of temporal good. He was to use it, but in subjecti onto higher, supersensuous realities. The discernment and maintenance of this law of subordination of the sensuous to the supersensuous was to constitute his perfection—it was his supreme law. The introduction of sin reversed this law—put the animal supreme and the spirit in subjection; put him under the dominion of the carnal mind and sensuous lusts, turned all his loves and desires toward the earth, made him dead to the supersensuous.

This is, and has been since the original severance of man from his Maker by disobedience, the estate of man by nature; that is, by birth. The animal essentially dominates him—he is by degeneracy "of the earth, earthy"—he delights in and lives for sensual pleasure. His sins all emanate from this source. He is not spiritually minded. Spiritual realities are undiscerned and unloved. The original law of his being is utterly broken. This is the fall of man—his depravity, his native sinfulness called. He is estranged from God and is immersed in fleshly lusts and sensualities—under the dominion of sensuous things.

It is a fact that the first attraction which reaches the soul on its entrance upon life is sensuous. As soon as it begins to live a conscious life or becomes able to feel an attraction it is drawn by and to the world and the flesh. As yet it has no idea of the supersensuous or spiritual. It has no proper rational life even. It is in an unethical state; that is, the ideas of right and wrong and obligation on the ethical ground of oughtness do not exist in it. Long before it reaches these ideas—the idea even that there are any spiritual realities or any moral laws—it has already become immersed in sensuosity; that is, its whole thought and affection and volitionating determine toward the earth. It is completely earth-bound. There is nothing else in the scope of its vision. It discovers in the world life in which it is bound things which powerfully attract it. There is no counter-attraction, for the supersensuous is wholly unknown. The earth spirit, which theologically takes the name of depravity, has complete sway in it. This is an important and indisputable fact.

But, meantime, in its deepest nature it is spiritual, and is made for another kind of life. The life it at present, that is, during the reign of sensuosity, lives is not altogether an alien life; it pertains to its constitution, but it is not its truest and best life; not the life that will ultimately develop in it, not the life it must permanently live. Under the film of sensuosity which now invests it there lies, without sign of life, a consciousness yet to be awakened toward an as yet unknown supersensuous world whose reality and power it will inevitably come to feel. In the core of its deepest, truest self is an ethic, a moral norm—a religion. When this hidden life shall begin to develop itself and its impulses shall begin to be felt, a new experience will develop in the soul, which will first appear as a schism, a discord, a warfare, as the pull of two conflicting attractions, one toward the objects which have hitherto swayed it, in which it has lived and found delight, and which have become masterful to it; another attraction toward objects and interest now for the first dimly discovered to it, but which press upon it and urge it as of supreme importance: the attractions of the supersensuous world; the sense of God; the pressure of a feeling of obligation toward him; the yearnings after something not given in sense; the indistinct outline of realities lying beyond time and away from the earth; voices calling to it, pleading with it, urging it—voices which it cannot hush. The ethical life begins.

It is in this innermost nature of the soul where Christian experiences are born. These are the first buddings, the dawning of the God consciousness, the germinations of the spiritual life. The antecedent life of sensualism inherited, while tending to sin and enslaving the soul up to the time when a higher consciousness is awakened, has no ethical character, and it never could acquire ethical character if the subject did not come to a state of knowledge in which he felt the obligation to bring it under law. There is no sin in an impulse of nature, no difference what it is, until it comes into relations with will and law.

However it became a fact, it is a fact that the human soul finds itself in the earliest stages of its etcical consciousness dead to spiritual realities. It is quite impossible to determine at what stage of life the soul comes to ethical consciousness. It is certainly not in early infancy. It doubtless varies in different cases: environments are influential and determining causes. With some ethical consciousness is awakened much earlier than with others. But, be it sooner or later, whenever the soul attains fully to that state it finds itself assuming an attitude of resistance to law, alive to evil lusts and sensuality, and opposed to whatever would restrain its wrong-going—

earthly, sensual, and devilish. Sin takes possession of it and makes it a willing slave. It is not wholly depraved, however; along with its first ethical consciousness it finds itself encompassed with redeeming influences. It discerns right and wrong. It becomes aware of something urging it to the right, for the divine Spirit meets its dawning consciousness. It is not wholly abandoned to evil. Its earthward and evil tendencies encounter opposition, but its inclination is to evil, and were it left wholly to itself, and environments without redeeming influences, it would immediately sink into loathsome sensuality and utter depravity: the impulses from within are all that way; and that it is not utterly lost and dead to righteousness is because redeeming influence reaches it. If the depraved impulses are restrained it is by gracious agency from without. It is early susceptible to the saving and restraining influences which come to it from the Holy Spirit. It may be early saved, before it comes to the consciousness of the power of evil within it, before it has acquired a relish for evil, and especially before it has come under the dominion of habits of sin; but in that case salvation must come from without. It cannot save itself.

This is the state and character of every human soul when it opens into ethical consciousness. Its first tendencies are earthward and evil, and without exceptions the tendencies ultimate in the actual sin as well as sinfulness of the soul. In a soul in this case Christianizing experiences take their rise. I do not doubt but that this statement will seem to put the soul at great disadvantage, and will seem to impeach God with ungenerous, if not unethical, treatment of it; nevertheless, that the statement is correct, accords with the facts, I do not doubt.

If we were compelled to accept the theological statement, long time persistently made, that the soul is rendered guilty by heredity, there would be some show of reason for the allegation that it takes its existence at great disadvantage, and would place the administration in an unvindicable light before the universe ; or if it could be shown that the mercy element introduced into the administration did not place the soul so marred on a fair footing for its personal probation, the same result would follow.

But if redemptive influences reach it in its new needs which more than counterbalance its injuries, then its marring would not be to its disadvantage. If it gains more in Christ than it lost in Adam its chances are improved.

The probation of an abnormal soul must, under a righteous administration, be planned in the recognition of that fact.

It is customary to assume—and it is not peculiar to any theological system, Arminianism and Calvinism in all their shades asserting it—that that Edenic probation, admitted to be perfectly fair, was a probation in which the eternal destiny of the subject was involved: Calvinism being responsible for the position that the subject included all the unborn souls of the human race, a pseudo-Arminianism not unfrequently expressing itself in a way that involves the same unethical idea : and as the probation issued in failure it is as constantly assumed by Calvinism that by the failure the guilty subject, including all humanity, was brought under condemnation to eternal death; Arminianism meanwhile, often by misstatement saving itself from the atrocious idea.

On this unethical basis Calvinism builds its entire system, so replete with horror that it makes one stand aghast to read it. I dare not pursue the subject further.

Before stating the true exposition of that ancient chapter of race history, I raise a question concerning that Adamic probation which, so far as I know, has not appeared in theological polemics upon that point. That question is this: Where does it appear in the Scriptures that the probation in which the Adam was placed was one which involved even his own eternal destiny? It is scripturally and historically certain that it did not, and we find ourselves compelled to affirm that there are ethical grounds why it could not. The revelation affirms that for that sin, and all other sins of men but that of a final irreversible self-determination to evil by any soul for itself, an anticipated remedy was already prepared before that first failure had occurred. The purpose of redemption antedated the fall. "The sacrificial lamb was in purpose slain from the foundation of the world." It was not an after-thought, an expedient to meet an unforeseen contingency. This is biblical, and it is also ethical.

The outcome of that Edenic chapter of probation and failure was not that the penalty of the law was executed upon the transgressor, if so be the penalty was eternal death. If it was eternal death it never was and never will be executed upon any soul of man. The sin of Eden did not send Adam to final perdition, and could not. That the penalty of eternal death was not executed could have been for no other reason than that it was not contentful to the divine nature that it should be— that is, the nature of God would not permit it. That he did not permit it is in proof that for some reason his nature would not permit it—could not on some immutable ethical grounds; for there could be no other reason. Let us search more narrowly into that chapter of probation and see if we cannot find an explanation that will shed light on the whole transaction. I am fully aware that I am attempting to tread a perilous edge, where great caution is necessary, and therefore ask critical attention to every point raised, that if error appears anywhere it may be pointed out. I think I am safe in saying that up to date no theological rendering of the Edenic case has been perfectly satisfactory, while some which have most widely prevailed, and continue to be put forward, with great but faltering persistence, have irrecoverably lost the respect of mankind. In substance, I believe our Wesleyan version of Arminianism has most nearly reached the solution, but with some marring, and with incidents of disharmony with itself, which more careful and critical statement may eliminate.

In the examination I start with the statement that I accept without reservation the historical account of the case made by Moses. I believe it is a true and divinely revealed account of the Edenic or Adamic probation. The search is as to exactly what the account contains, in the light of fundamental ethics, and subsequent history, and revelations that have a bearing on the subject.

The account given by Moses is the simplest possible. This is its great merit. There is nothing *outré* or mysterious about it. The circumstances are natural and intelligible. It has all the appearance of a plain unvarnished story. It commends itself as probable. There is nothing in human knowledge of an historical, rational, scientific, or ethical kind to throw doubt upon it. The deepest philosophy suggests no improvement of it. It claims to have been received from God. The subject-matter is such as to exclude the possibility of any other authorship on any other theory than that it is fiction of human invention. Of this there is no evidence and much disproof.

The law was the simplest possible, but it served as a moral test—that is, the test whether the subject would obey law. That was what it was for. It perfectly answered its end. Would a more complex and difficult law have been better? Who will affirm it, considering the circumstances of the case?

The law forbade that which something in the nature of the subject craved. This is important to be noted. Could it have been a moral test without that? Could it have been less and answer the end of determining character?

The outcome was that the subject chose unrighteousness. Simple as the test was he did not endure it. I am willing to say, in order to give all possible strength to the case, that it was foreknown that he would fail. This fact must be taken into the account in order to the explanation of the whole case, and must give complexion to it. I cannot here enter into the polemic or foreknowledge further than to say that it had no influence whatever as causing the act of disobedience, but *it was* influential as affecting the administration with respect to the act of disobedience. The whole subject in all its bearings is fully discussed in the treatises already referred to. We have now reached the point in the history where objection springs. It is said the subject, considering his inexperience, never should have been placed in a situation of such imminent peril. The objection is purely instinctive. Has it been considered what the position means? Can there be an ethical system without such peril? What is righteous character but the free choice of right with the possible choice of wrong? To assume that no subject should be placed in such condition of peril as to possibly make a wrong choice is simply to assert that a moral universe ought not to exist. That depends on what the foreknown outcome will be. It is perfectly safe to affirm that its existence, caused by a holy and loving God, is stronger proof that it ought to exist than any evidence to the contrary from purely instinctive judgment of any finite creature.

But it is said that the foreknowledge of failure in this case at least ought to have estopped the peril. That depends on two things; namely, how this particular history stands related to the whole ethical system in all time and over all worlds, and what else was foreknown of the outcome of this trial.

But it is said in any event the treatment of the subject is inexcusably severe. Infinite love ought to have interfered. Here, again, we have the cry of the she wolf—mere instinct without reason.

Has the case been severely treated? I am sure that justice never has been done to this question. Let us calmly look at it in a changed form. How ought it to have been treated and how has it been treated? Is there ground for the charge of severity? I am sure that any thing like a fair examination will secure the verdict that the treatment has been the tenderest possible—the treatment of unsurpassed and unsurpassable love.

What are the facts? Was the culprit dealt with harshly? Was he driven away in wrath to irrecoverable doom? Was he consigned to remediless sin and everlasting torments? Were his unborn descendants left to welter in the horrors of inevitable sin and shame as the result of his inexcusable deed? Where is it said? Shall we forever continue to asperse God and pervert the plainest statements of history at the dictation of a false human creed on the one hand, or the mere ebullitions of unreasoning instinct on the other? Is there to be no limit to the blasphemy against infinite love?

What says the history? Does it not faithfully record that, foreseeing the calamity, infinite love had already provided a remedy? Does it not show that the probation, instead of being ended and the case finally adjudicated, was only begun? the first chapter merely of continuous history? Would it not be wiser to be at the pains to read the history through?

The story is a pathetic one. It reveals to us a loving father dealing with an erring and wayward child—the more you put in the sin of the child the greater the tenderness of compassion on the part of the father. A grievous wrong had been committed—a tragedy of evil initiated—the peace of the universe disturbed, not by the eating of an apple, as fools flippantly assert, but by an act of disobedience which involved the choice of evil instead of good; which changed the character of the transgressing child; which changed his relations to law; which immutable ethics demanded should be recognized in the aftertreatment of the transgressor; which no power could obliterate; which to remedy would cost an infinite price of suffering and sorrow. We stand at the open door of the greatest tragedy of all time. The guilty culprit, who, willingly or not, had opened the "Pandora's box" and let loose the fiends of evil to raven and destroy, stands before whom? An inexorable, an unrelenting judge? A frowning, lowering, omnipotent vengeance? No, not that; but before a holy and compassionate father, compelled to deal with his offending child but moved with pity and intent on remedy rather than punishment; not moved more by justice than by love—more by justice tempered by love. Compassion intones the entire narrative. He reproves but he comforts. Could he have done less? At what infinite cost he undertakes to remedy the breach!

What was the result? The sin had been committed; it could not be recalled. Neither the sinning child nor sinned-against parent had power to obliterate it. It must be dealt with as sin. This immutable ethics demanded.

The culprit was marred in character, the evil of sin had gone into his soul; but it was by his own choice. He was turned out of Paradise. It was prepared for the sinless. He had sinned. Was a wrong done him in sending him away? To assume it is to assume that the sinning and the sinful should have no different treatment—again the cry of the she wolf; instinct against reason.

I ask critical attention to the further statement I now make.

Though turned out of Paradise, with a character marred and with a nature perverted by his sin, the culprit was not forsaken but was permitted to live under a prolonged probation—the continued probation mercifully adapted to his altered circumstances.

It was not now a probation of an innocent person to test whether under temptation he would choose evil instead of good. That test had been already passed and he had determined himself to evil.

It was not a probation to test whether, now that he had become guilty, he would reconsider and restore himself to righteousness. That was impossible. Guilt once incurred cannot purge itself. The sinner cannot annihilate the fact of his sin nor remove its guilt by any atonement he can offer or reparation he can make.

It was not a probation under which, by a sovereign act, the culprit was forgiven or placed under a less rigorous law. The law could not be relaxed; it can require nothing less than righteousness and absolute obedience. Nor can there be an act of sovereign forgiveness for its violation. Under continued probation the law is neither abolished nor modified, and under it there is no sovereign forgiveness.

It was not a probation under which incurred guilt was imputed to another and the righteousness of another imputed to the culprit. Though a probation under unrelaxed law it was not a probation under law alone, in which failure in a single case, or even many grievous and continuous failures, closed the test and consigned the culprit to the doom of final and irretrievable ruin. I call special attention to this statement.

The probation was that of a guilty sinner, made such by his own free choice of evil under the most favorable opportunity and highest motives to the choice of good; of a sinner who by his sin had not only incurred guilt but had thereby introduced into his nature a perverting habit and tendency to evil which bound him to perpetual sinning so far as any power himself possessed. A soul touched with the virus of sin cannot cure itself. There is in it no power of self-redemption. This it is that makes the deepest evil of sin.

It is obvious that probation to such a soul, were there nothing more to be said, would be meaningless. Where there is only one possible outcome, what the end will be is determined before the trial.

We add, therefore, it was the probation of a guilty and sinful soul under the provisions of an atonement originated not by itself but by the infinite love against which it had sinned; an atonement which was to be wrought out at a great price of suffering voluntarily endured on its behalf; an atonement under which its sin, and any and all sins it might commit, might be forgiven, and its blighted and perverted nature be restored to normalcy, on one condition: that it should yield to the mighty persuasions of love under helpful influences of a regenerating power ever at hand, which enable it to renounce its sin and sue for pardon.

I cannot here enter at all into the polemic of that atonement in any aspect of it as to its extent or the why of its efficacy, but rest the statement here, with the assertion of the fact that there was such an atonement made for the sinning Adam and for all of his posterity covering their sin, and that continued probation is under its provisions.

Does this look like severity? Does it reveal to us a character inexorable and unrelenting—an unforgiving vengeance as seated on the throne of the universe? Is it hard treatment to ask a sinner to renounce his sins and sue for pardon? Is it hard treatment to provide an atonement for him at the greatest possible cost when he was too poor and helpless to provide one for himself? Is it hard treatment to bear with him through years of impenitence and insolent wickedness, persuading and entreating him not to destroy himself? Is it hard treatment to enlist all possible influences to save him—to move heaven and earth on his behalf? Is it hard treatment if, after all possible efforts to save him he is still found to be impenitent, and has made for himself the irreversible choice of evil, to send him away to his own place? Where else should he be sent? What other disposition could be made of him? If when the probation ends it is because character has assumed an unchangeable type by the irreversible choice of evil, and if at the end destiny is determined by fixed and incorrigible impenitence self-elected, under all the circumstances investing the trial who but a devil dare accuse the ever blessed God with having been unmerciful? Who can name any thing that should have been done that has not been done?

In passing away from the chapter of initial probation in Eden I affirm that neither Adam nor any one of his posterity ever was damned to eternal and irretrievable death for the sin which he then committed.

I further affirm that no such result followed the act, because the nature of God was such that he could not permit it—such that he never proposed any thing of the kind—and not because of any change of mind arising from unexpected exigencies.

I affirm yet further that the act of Eden did change the relations between God and the sinning Adam, and did radically affect the nature of Adam, introducing into his soul a tendency to sin which he, left to himself, had no power to reverse.

I affirm that this new but foreseen condition of things was the basis of an atonement scheme antedating the sin, by which probation was continued and under which eternal destiny is administered.

I affirm that Adam's sin in the breach of the Eden law, and all other sins that he ever committed, were his own sins, and nobody else's, and that there never was or could be a sharer in his guilt; and, therefore, that the atonement provided was not an atonement for the guilt of any one of his posterity with respect to that act, since they were not, and could not be, guilty concerning it.

I affirm still yet further that such are the relations of Adam and his posterity that, by heredity and natural descent, the marring which sin brought into his nature is transmitted to his posterity, and that all born of him receive from him a fatal bias to sin such that not one of his line has ever escaped it; and such that, but for the restoring agencies which emanate from the atonement under which they take their existence, they would be involved in utter ruin; and, therefore, such as would have prevented their existence had no provision been prepared and made for its remedy.

I affirm yet once more that while hereditary depravity does not involve guilt on the part of those who receive it, either for the sin which introduced it or on its own account, it is an evil which must be removed; and that the atonement provides for its removal or deliverance from its power on the same conditions on which personal sins are forgiven—regeneration and forgiveness being concomitant of the same act of justification by which a sinner becomes a child of God and heir of eternal life.

LECTURE 4.

PROCESS AND ELEMENTS OF EXPERIENCE. FORGIVENESS.

We have seen now how sin was introduced, that is, how man came under the miseries of sin. It is not our business in these lectures to more than state these scriptural deliverances. We find the fact of sin; this is God's explanation of its origin. We assert that no other account ever has been given, or ever can be given, which does not make God the direct author of sin, and make him solely responsible for it. These facts show that God is responsible for creating the possibility of sin, but that man is responsible for creating the fact of sin against God's expressed prohibition and desire. This statement is intended in all its inclusions to be exact. There is a measure of responsibility on the part of God which must enter into his treatment of sin, for the possibility of which his creative act had prepared the way. Let us try to find just what that measure of responsibility is, and just how it must influence his administration.

This will appear if we reflect: (a) he made the subject so that he could sin—if he had not so done there could have been no sin; (b) he placed him in conditions where he would be exposed to the temptation to sin—if he had not so done there would have been no sin; (c) he foresaw that he would sin. Of these facts there can be no doubt, and in his own account of it they are not disguised but are fully stated. Under the light of these facts his administration must be vindicated before the universe. His holiness, which is but another name for the infinite purity of his justice and love, is involved.

If the circumstances of the trial were fair up to the point where sin emerged there can be no real ground of fault in the divine proceeding up to that point. But an absolute prerequisite to that is that the trial should have been perfectly fair; that is, that the subject of the trial had complete and adequate power to know and do what was required. It may be well to linger for a moment here. If he create a moral being at all he must involve the possibility of sin. The one is the inclusion of the other. It was, therefore, the alternative of no moral universe or the possibility of sin. Any plan of creation which would exclude a moral universe, that is, a universe with persons, would reduce him to the necessity of making a universe simply of things, with no minds to enjoy it and no ethical or intellectual good to be enjoyed; a universe, therefore, with no other significance than simply a meaningless exhibition of power for himself to contemplate—a universe that could display no attribute of either justice or love or the infinite perfection of holiness in any form, and from which all ethical enjoyment must be excluded.

If he create moral beings he must put them under moral laws. That which his conjoint attributes of justice and love require—attributes never separated or separable in administration over finite moral beings—is that he enact laws obedience to which would express loyalty to essential righteousness, and disobedience to which would involve the essence of willful sin. For such disobedience he must enact suitable penalties, both as incentives to obedience and as expressing his own righteousness. Such laws must be level to the comprehension of the creature or they would be as unjust as unmerciful. The law must demand nothing difficult of obedience to the subject in view of his measure of ability; it must, in other words, be adjusted to the kind of faculty he possessed and the precise environments in which he was placed, so as neither to be oppressive or difficult. It must furnish him a fair and perfectly equitable chance to secure all the good of obedience and avert all the evils of disobedience. Nothing short of this would render it possible to vindicate the character of the Creator. And up to the point of the occurrence of sin these facts would furnish a perfect vindication.

Allow now that he knew that the perfectly fair trial would issue in disobedience, does this circumstance in any way affect the question of how he should administer on its occurrence? We are compelled to answer affirmatively. In the first place we are compelled to answer that such foreknowledge of the outcome, while it is admitted that it would not lessen the crime of disobedience, as mere foreknowledge would in no way be causative of the act; and while it would in no way render the trial unfair, it must do one of two things—namely, (*a*) either it must estop the creative act because of the evil outcome foreknown, or (*b*) it must require the introduction of an element of mercy into the administration by which pardon would be possible, or the character of God must be forever unvindicable before the universe. We assert this, with whatever it involves, not merely as probable, but as absolutely certain and ethically necessary, and we linger for a moment for its defense. That God himself so viewed it is apparent in the fact that he did, on the occurrence of the sin, introduce the mercy element in the administration, and in the further fact that he purposed so to do before the creative act. That he did so do he declares himself. And that he prepurposed so to do was not an unethical purpose, but was so because his ethical nature demanded it—because he could not be the eternally holy God, that is, the eternally just and loving God, and not do it. The fact that he did so do, and prepurposed so to do, prove that it was according to his nature to do it, and that not to do it would have been contrary to his nature. This is a sufficient answer, but it may be useful to state the underlying principles which must have so determined him. The question whether he would create a moral being who he knew would sin against him, and who he knew on the occurrence of sin would become accursed, was one touching his free act. Now, the determination of that question how he would act must depend upon what would be the outcome of the act of the creature he was to make. If he knew perfectly that it would issue only in curse is it possible to reconcile it to any thing that we are compelled to think of God that he would proceed to create with no alternative in his mind as the means of averting the curse? What could move him to the act? What end of justice would be served? What end of his own glory in any possible aspect? By supposition he perfectly knew that only one result would issue; that, the eternal and remediless curse of the creature he made. The thought that he would proceed with this only alternative is blasphemous. If this were the only alternative present to his thought every attribute of his nature must revolt against the creative act.

But suppose now that he foresaw the sin and the incurrence of its penalty, and along with it purposed immediately to introduce redemption, at once the question, Shall he proceed to create? has another aspect—a new line of administration places the question whether he will create or not in a new light.

The knowledge that the creation of a free being must involve the possibility of sin, and the foreknowledge that the possibility would certainly ripen into reality, and the knowledge that the reality would expose the culprit to curse and ruin, in the absence of any plan to avert the calamity, must inevitably have arrested the creative act, unless some remedy was seen to be possible. But allow the prepurpose to furnish such a remedy, would then either justice or love now stand in the way of procedure? Would not both of these eternally co-working attributes unite to impel to the creative act? To this question there can be but one answer; that is, that in the degree in which a personal universe is more to be desired than a mere universe of things it would be wise to proceed.

But still the question would emerge, Suppose that it was foreknown that the remedy provided would not be entirely effectual; that some among myriads would reject and remain under curse; what then? The question is a fair one, and to it we have to answer: The case must be reviewed in connection of the entire ethical system.

We think it is safe to assume that if God foresaw that the moral system would issue only in disaster he could not on any ethical principles have created a moral system. It is impossible to conceive infinite goodness as creating when it was foreknown no good, and only evil, would inevitably, or even certainly, result from his act. The same principle applies to any one individual in the moral system if so be the particular individual could be estopped from existence without involving the destruction of a paramount good. But if it was foreknown that among a vast number of beings under moral conditions some would certainly bring evil upon themselves, but that the vast majority would attain to the greatest felicity; and if it were impossible to eliminate the evil without at the same time preventing the good, it cannot be shown upon any ethical grounds that the good ought to be deprived of existence in order to prevent the self-incurred evil of the few who would come to grief under the system.

All that can be required for the perfect vindication of infinite goodness is that the system adopted should be the best possible, securing the greatest amount of good attainable, and reducing the evil to the lowest minimum. This his own ethical nature must require. If it were possible for him to keep out all evil without also preventing a paramount good his nature would require this.

Should it be foreknown that evil would arise under the system his whole ethical nature, justice as much as love, would put a demand on him to limit it as much as possible by the employment of all possible agencies for its extirpation. The necessary outcome of his proceeding must be that he did all possible to prevent evil finding an entrance into the system, and, after it made its appearance, every thing possible to extirpate it, short of a method that would involve still greater evil by eliminating all possible good, or the greatest possible good.

It is in the light of these principles that we must judge of and interpret his proceedings with man, and especially the workings of the remedial system.

But some one is ready to say: Had not God power to prevent evil from invading the universe? To say he had not, is it not to limit his omnipotence? To this question we answer in two parts: (*a*) He had the power to prevent evil by not creating a moral universe. If he might omit that there would be no evil. But could he, as the infinitely good and holy, omit it? (*b*) But could he not have made a moral system with only good in it? We answer, Yes; that was precisely the moral system he did make. There was no evil in any thing that he made. But had he not power to prevent it from being introduced? To this we answer again in two parts: (*a*) Power cannot prevent a moral creature from going wrong except by de-ethicalizing him, that is, by overthrowing his ethical nature. Ethical acts are not preventable by power; but (*b*) if he could prevent it how is it to be accounted for that he permits it on any other principle than that he prefers it on its own account, or because there is a paramount good in it? which is a contradiction.

It is easy to folly and effrontery to say: Why, if God is displeased with sin, did he not prevent it, and if he desires to get clear of it why does he not banish it? But this is mere ebullition of ignorance—the cry of the she wolf.

The answer to all such inane blasphemy is: Sin is here because man chooses to sin. It is here, not because God is pleased to have it, but because men are pleased to commit it. He did not and does not prevent it because he does not choose to abolish men and a moral universe, and because he has no power to prevent it if free beings choose to have it. His law and the sinless system he created represent his feeling with regard to it. The plan of rescue from it expresses his desire to get rid of it. If there were any other possible, more effectual way, it is certain that he would have adopted that.

Sin is here by choice of man. It is found to be the most patent and the most potent fact in human history, and, we may be bold to say, the most dreadful fact in the entire history of the universe. No one disputes it. Its fell shadow falls athwart the entire history of the race. Its malign and awful presence reveals itself in every soul of man. It is unmixed evil, and portentous of still deeper evil. This statement accords with every consciousness. It carries terror to every reflecting mind. It projects its portentous gloom over a possible immortality. Only fools make light of it.

To the question, How shall it be dealt with? what will be the outcome? the guilt-smitten soul returns only the dumb answer of instinct. The spontaneous first thought is to appease avenging wrath which it feels lowering over it. All heathenism is the exponent of this thought. All its rites and offerings are peace-offerings—appeasements. The entire history of heathenism proclaims man's consciousness of guilt and dread of vengeance—his hopeless impotence cowering before the terrors of retributive wrath; the impossibility of self-deliverance but the inevitability of the effort. No offering can appease avenging justice while sin remains. Justice cannot be bought off. The thing God hates is sin. The blood of bulls and goats, and more costly offerings, is not what he wants. They are nothing to him. What is wanted is salvation from sin. That will stay all penalty—nothing else can. No human effort that comes short of this is of any avail. The problem is how to get rid of sin. That solved, all else is easy. Sacrifices do not put it away. No sacrifice; not even the great sacrifice God himself provided. No sacrifice appeases. What is wanted is not appeasement; it is the removal of sin. This can never be done in any other way than by inducing the sinner to renounce it: In order to that he must be revolutionized—made over.

As any sacrifices he may offer cannot do that, so also he cannot revolutionize himself. He has no power to do it in himself. Here is where the religion of culture is a failure. Culture cannot remove guilt. Culture cannot change the nature. These are the things that are wanted. Sin kills. What is needed is a power to make alive.

Failing to appease avenging wrath by any thing it can do, and failing to be able to restore itself by any thing that it can do—hopelessly guilty, bound hand and foot to evil, smitten with despair—the affrighted soul turns upon its Maker and Sovereign and accuses him as a merciless tyrant. In vain does Sovereignty reply: Is not the law just? Does it require any thing oppressive? Is it not beneficent as well as just? Would not obedience to it have worked for the highest welfare? Does not its transgression work endless harm and misery? As a loving sovereign was I not bound to make such a law? Would

I have been guiltless had I made any other law less perfect? Can I be just or true to the creatures I have made and permit it to be set aside and trampled on? Am I not bound to secure the good it provides for by compelling it to be respected by enforcing its sanctions? Were not you fully warned of the consequences of transgression? Was not your disobedience a free voluntary act? Is not the harm that comes to you in its penalties of your own procuring? Can you with reason or justice complain of me for your self-incurred evil by the perverse and willful abuse of what I intended for your good? The defense seems to be fair. There is not one of the allegations implied against which a word can be said.

But despite the defense the affrighted soul feels that, dealt with on these principles of rigorous justice, it is the victim of a great wrong—the justice is too severe to be just, even; in its unrelenting rigors it overleaps itself and becomes stained—justice, pure and simple, unmixed with mercy toward a finite and fallable creature, becomes cruelty. The soul continues its plea. It says, allow that justice condemns with justice, yet the thing is wrong. The injustice lies further back, in giving me existence and placing me in exposedness to such a fate. It is cruelty to create a fallable creature and place him under circumstances where he may, however freely, incur remediless evil upon a single chance. I had no choice in my creation. Your sovereign act placed me here in being. You made me what I am. Had it been possible to know these grievous possibilities, and had I been allowed a choice, I would have preferred not to be. It was an act of pure and cruel despotism that made me under conditions that have brought these evils upon me. There is not even the excuse of good intention marred by unforeseen contingencies. Thou knewest even when creating me what the outcome was sure to be. Waxing still more bold, the defiant, not merely affrighted and helpless, soul continues its plea. Looking Sovereignty in the face it says: I never had a chance; I was sent here maimed—a hopeless cripple, with impossibility to do otherwise than sin. The blight of another's curse for his own sin, not mine, reached me in the womb ere I was born, and so warped my faculties that escape from this curse which I now suffer was never in my reach. I am foredoomed by the sin of another, of which my sins are unfree accidents however they seem to be my free and personal acts.

To this impeachment there is and can be no answer if we suppose the divine government based and administered on the principle of abstract and absolute justice alone which renders penalty irremissible if the subject is to be such a subject as man. With such a subject there can be no irremissible penalty for sin. There may be penalty eternally inflicted but it must be remissible penalty. That it continues forever must not be because he who executes it could not and would not remit it, but because he who suffers it has finally and irreversibly rejected the merciful conditions on which alone it could be remitted. The penalty abides because the sinner has irreversibly and freely determined the rejection of proffered pardon, fixing himself in sin, and not because it is *de facto* irremissible.

In recognizing the principle of mercy and possible pardon, and in providing for it in actual administration, which all admit, God himself shows that the actual administration is not on the principle of abstract and absolute justice alone, and is not so because it ought not, that is, ethically could not, be so carried on. The mercy which he introduced was not unethical, but what, was obligatory on him as an immutable ethical principle of his nature; as much so as that of justice itself. Grace is his free act, but not, therefore, in contravention with ethical obligation. He could no more administer without mercy than without justice.

Mercy must not be in contravention of justice, and no more can justice be in contravention of mercy. The two eternal and immutable attributes must be administratively harmonious. The law in all of its requirements and sanctions must accord with perfect justice, for he cannot be in conflict with justice. It must be administered in mercy, but not at the sacrifice of the principle of justice, for he cannot be less than merciful. This was the great problem, the greatest of all problems, for the Infinite to solve. To the impeachment of ignorant fright and terror the infinite heart of love replies: "It is not so. The case is not at all as you put it; it is the extremest opposite. If my dealing with you were as you assume, though you are a worm, and even on the ground that you are a worm and I the Almighty, your accusation would be just. I should then deserve the execration of every creature in the universe. I should not be able to think of myself but with abhorence. If there is a single creature in the wide realm of existence whom I have treated as you allege you have been treated, no matter what his sin, my infamy were greater than that of devils. But you are mistaken. The indictment is false in all of its essential and malign features. This is what is true: I did permit you to be brought into existence with a marred nature whose tendencies are to evil. It is also true that it is by reason of no fault of yours that you are so marred. It is further true that you have no power to remedy the marring of nature which comes to you by inheritance. It is also true that your personal sins have had their source in the natural depravity which was propagated in you without your consent. So much I am compelled to admit. If now the defense stopped here nothing is more certain than that the indictment would stand in every feature of it. But infinite love proceeds with its defense: It is not true that I have ever accounted you guilty, or that I have ever proposed to punish you for the nature you inherit, or that I have required of you the impossible thing of rectifying it by your unaided self-power. It is not true that I have left you to the inevitable punishment of your sins personally committed by the free choice of evil, even. It is not true that I have cruelly forsaken you in your sad and helpless condition and left you to your self-chosen wickedness. What is true is, I have ever been a pitying Father. In your helplessness I have laid help upon One mighty to save; I have borne with you; I have provided for you full and ample opportunities to make your existence one of immeasurable blessedness. This is the one thing I have constantly sought in all my dealings with you. I have made infinite sacrifice for you; I have employed all possible influences to save you; I have offered forgiveness on the single condition that you renounce your sins; I have persuaded and entreated you. If finally you are lost it will be after all efforts to save you have been unavailing, and then only because when it was fully in your power, made so by unsolicited help, you have rejected offered mercy and have of your own volition irreversibly elected evil instead of good. I call the universe to witness that I have exhausted the resources of infinite love. What could I have done that I have not done?"

This defense accords with the exact facts; and that it is a perfect defense no spirit in the universe can gainsay. Love intones all the proceedings of God with respect to man from the beginning to the end. There is not a chapter from the opening chapter in Eden, not an incident to the closing chapter of eternal doom, that does not reveal infinite love as presiding over the destinies of men.

LECTURE 5.

ELEMENTS OF EXPERIENCE.

The preceding discussions have sufficiently developed the principles and the facts of administration under which Christian experience emerges; that it is the experience of a soul under a beneficent probation, under which every soul of man has a fair chance to secure to itself a happy immortality.

The discussion first disclosed how man became involved in sin, and then unfolded the method by which infinite love seeks to deliver him from sin by a continued probation under redemptive influences and agencies. It further developed that in the entire history and providential plan of proceeding there is nothing arbitrary, or artificial, or merely volitional on the part of God, but that the whole proceeding has been and is conducted on the immutable ethic of the divine nature.

I deem it important, before stating the facts of experience which in their wholeness constitute Christian experience, to state once more that they are facts which do not emerge in the soul by its own agency alone, nor by the agency of God alone, but by the concurrence and coaction of God the Father, God the Son, and God the Holy Ghost—the Trinity in the Godhead—with the soul.

I reaffirm also that God in Trinity has no power to recover the sinful and guilty soul without its coaction. This may seem like a bold statement, but a moment's reflection, without argument, will justify it. If it were possible to Godhead to save the soul without its coaction, then all souls would be brought to the experience of salvation if it were not that God did not wish to save them; for if he could work salvation in one without his coaction, he could work salvation in all without their coaction. The explanation why some will not be saved is not that God did not choose to save some, and did choose to save others; but because some souls determined, by a free, irreversible choice, not to be saved.

This position is essential to the philosophy of Christian experience, and is important to be emphasized, because of a long time vicious theologizing, which ascribes every thing in salvation—that is, in Christian experience—to the direct and sovereign act of God on the souls of a certain number called the elect, or to an irresistible efficacy in means employed. In either form the idea is unethical and false. Nothing done by God, either through or without the atonement, ever did or ever can save a responsible human soul without its own coaction.

The truth is, God seeks to save all men, and out of his infinite love, self-moved, has provided means and a method of salvation, which include conditions to be performed freely by man; and among these means are the atonement (atonement is only a means) wrought by Christ, and a revelation of that fact to man, accompanied with instructions, invitations, and promises, and with helpful influences of the Holy Ghost, empowering, but not coercing, man to comply with the conditions. Until the conditions are complied with salvation is not effected. When man performs his part God saves him; that is, brings him into the full and completed experience of salvation. Thus God and man are co-factors. The whole scheme of salvation is to be interpreted in the light of this principle, and it is fatal to the whole scheme of election and all the unethical postulates and warnings connected therewith, and the doctrine of atonement built thereon.

Before more specifically naming and elaborating the several separate elements of Christian experience, we call attention to the fact that there is an exact and logical order in which these elementary parts emerge. The order is philosophical; that is, rational; it never is and cannot be inverted. Each incident occupies the precise place it must occupy to accord with the mental and moral constitution of the soul, and each incident has a differentiable conditioning ground. The experience is a unity out of severalty, each incident of which is necessary to the completed whole—nothing can be transposed or omitted, though the experience may be intermitted at any point short of completion—the beginning does not necessarily carry with it the end. The end is only secured by the soul freely complying with the conditions until the end is reached. No soul ever did or ever can comply with the conditions throughout and the end fail.

Christian experience is absolute proof of the truth of Christianity. There is perfect harmony between the experience and the entire code of doctrines in the Christian system. All the doctrines have bearing in some way on the experience. The experience is Christianity incarnated—concrete experience of it.

What are the elements of Christian experience? In the present lecture they will be named and explained in the order of their occurrence.

We are now prepared to take up and examine the facts of Christian experience. There are elements in Christian experience that are common to all men, which therefore exist where no completed Christian experience exists, but without which there is *no* Christian experience; which, therefore, must be taken account of in any adequate statement of the constitutive elements of Christian experience. The beginnings of grace are revealed in every adult human soul. These primary and initial experiences constitute the conditioning grounds of all subsequent experiences, without which they would be impossible; they furnish the necessary bases of all after stages. They are of divine emanation. The human soul has no power to lift itself to God, if God do not first condescend to it. It must forever remain in the sensuosity into which it is fallen, did not God lift it up out of the abysm by some helpful movement upon it, enabling it to coact with him. This is called initial grace.

Divine illumination is the first element in any soul's *de facto* redemption—its first redemptive experience. This is vouchsafed in a degree to every human soul. There is a divine "light that lighteneth every man that cometh into the world," which is sufficient, if followed, to lead it to its fountain and source, so that there is no absolute necessity that any soul of man should be lost. But the light which shines dimly in the benighted chambers of a heathen soul, while it may lead it to the everlasting fountain of light and life, is not adequate to a *Christian* experience. There must be added supernatural revelation. The light which shines from the holy pages of revelation and from the holy character of Jesus of Nazareth furnishes the divine illumination which is necessary to the dawn of *Christian* experience. Through these God comes to the sensualized soul, and by their shining lights up the supersensuous and unseen, as nature and the Spirit in the use of mere nature do not. In their shining the powers of the invisible world appear—the soul discerns itself and its law—the path of duty and of life is made plain to it. The divine illumination thus projected into the soul becomes matter of consciousness. Under it all things appear in a new light; that which was before in a haze of uncertainty becomes real; faith in the supersensible is born. It is the first end of "the path that shineth more and more unto the perfect day." It is a holy light, and it reveals the "holy of holies"—the holiness of God, the holiness of heaven, and the great fact that nothing unholy can enter therein. The human soul, under divine illumination, becomes conscious of a law revealed to it which demands holiness. The heavenly light opens upon it ineffable sanctities.

Conviction, the second stage of experience, is born. The illuminated soul, under the heavenly shining, discovers that it is utterly defiled. Patent as that fact now becomes to its consciousness, but for that opening to it of the holy of holies it could never have made the discovery. To a soul that has closed its doors against the shining of that holy light sin seems a trivial thing—an accident or mistake merely—a passing misconduct—a happening that has no deep significance, which comes to the earthly life of man and makes a momentary stain, may be, but which time and other experiences will efface; but, to one who has seen God in his revelation, who has passed through into the inner shrine of the divine sanctities, that has seen the veil uplifted, and through the veil has beheld the unspeakable vision of stainless and immaculate purities—the effulgence of a holiness before which even the heavens are stained and angels are charged with folly—a blaze of righteousness which consumes all iniquity—sin becomes exceeding sinful, a very tragedy of evil. That such is the eternal holiness of God is the burden of revelation; the express teaching is, that he cannot look upon sin with allowance—that it is the one thing which his nature abhors with unmitigated loathing.

In the light of this revelation the illuminated soul sees itself, and there is borne in upon it the sense of utter guilt and defilement. The eternal ethic slays it. To it sin is never again mere petty delinquencies—mere external follies and foibles—the ephemeral incidents or escapades of transient thoughtlessness. The blaze of day has penetrated its innermost consciousness, and the holy law lays itself along-side of the habitual thoughts and desires and purposes which are found there, and the discovery is made to it that itself is shot through and through with the deadly virus—that itself is rotten and leprous, a filthy cage of reptiles and unclean birds, that it is evil and only evil, and that continually—that its very sanctities are unholy lusts. It sums up its whole moral consciousness in one word: "Unclean, unclean, unclean." No soul has ever seen itself in the light of revelation, or in the light of true self-knowledge, that will not recognize the realism of this dreadful picture.

There is a general vague sense of sin which all men feel. Under redemption no soul of man is or can be without this. It emerges in the dimmest twilight of ethical consciousness. It brings to the soul disquiet and unrest, unsatisfiedness with itself, weariness with its state, the dull pain of a diseased nerve; but it is often for a time, and possibly on account of personal delinquency forever, kept under opiates or drowned with dissipations or eager pursuits of pleasure or business. It is incipient but smothered conviction.

The grace of thorough awakening, when admitted to the soul—that is, when the soul yields its consent to look at itself in the light of the divine law—is a great uplift toward spiritual life, the beginning of a great experience, often alarming and deeply painful at first, but always medicative, healing, the bursting open of the door for the in-coming of a celestial guest.

It is not pretended that in every case of genuine Christian experience there is the same degree of vivid consciousness of the utter corruption of the heart or the same phenomena of self-accusing. Personal history accounts for wide diversity; but a sense of guilt is a universal concomitant of all Christian experience. Many times the divine illumination brings out into startling prominence some one act of enormous sin and fixes the gaze of the soul exclusively upon it, and impales, transfixes it with the single fact. Many times it is a long line of criminal offenses, a life-time of sins, that is held before its gaze. Again, it is simple conviction of neglect, ingratitude, unworthiness; but it must be conviction of sin, consciousness of guilt, if the soul is ever to rise out of it into a sense of pardon. Sinfulness emerges as ground of condemnation.

Now it is possible to conceive of the soul's experience stopping here. There is no absolute necessity in the nature of the soul that it should ever pass from under or beyond this experience. We should then have a soul forever self-condemned and gnawed with perpetual remorse, or a dead or a lost soul. Itself could never abolish the fact of its guilt. The law which condemns it could never be reversed, for it is an immutable law. Its condemnation must be perpetual and its remorse everlasting—the inextinguishable fire and the deathless worm, the hell of the Bible. If we suppose the process to stop here, conviction is not an element of Christian experience, but an element of the experience of a lost soul that might have led on to Christian experience. To raise conviction to the quality of an element of grace, and thus bring it into the line of saving experience, it must condition a further experience.

We have said that the soul has no power to reverse the facts and lift itself out from under the condemnation which kills it. If now we suppose God to be moved with pity at its forlorn condition, and by as imperative a law as the law of holiness itself we are compelled to think he was, and could not but be, so moved (and this intuitive judgment is shown to be true by his own revelation, for he declares that he was so moved with pity), the question emerges, how could pity become available to remedy the case?

It is certain that there are some things which God, however moved by pity, could not do. He could not reverse his own law without subverting his own immaculate holiness, for his law is the simple exponent and expression of his holiness. He could not change the fact of sin. It is not in the power of God even to make that not a fact which is a fact. He could not ignore the fact and treat the guilty sinner as if he were not a sinner; for that would require him to subvert the ethic of his own nature by making no distinction between righteousness and unrighteousness. He could not force a reversal of character in the sinner himself; for that would be to reduce the sinner from a person to a thing, and so to violate the law of his personality. These are things which we know could not be. And yet we know just as certainly as we know any one of these facts that mercy is one of the eternal attributes of his nature, precisely as we know that justice is.

The law convicts of sin, and still sets forth its unabated command—relaxes nothing. There is no salvation by the law. But so there is no salvation without it. It must do its work. It must convince of sin, whether the sinner be saved or not. If punished, it must be with the knowledge and consciousness of sin. If saved, it must also be after the knowledge and deep consciousness of sin. Without this consciousness it is impossible that it should be brought forward into other experiences which are necessary to the experience of pardon.

That the process do not stop here it is requisite there should be further illumination by a further revelation. The law is not sufficient. Up to this stage the soul stands before the external and internal Sinai—the eternal law and inexorable justice. The revelation transfixes with terror—slays it. There is nothing else that it can do. No sound of mercy intones condemning law. Its only sentence is: "The soul that sinneth, it shall die." It provides for no pardons. It inspires no hope. It relentlessly kills. The glare of its awful light smites with despair and death. The eternal ethic of the divine nature requires that it should be so.

But, then, is there no salvation? None by the way of Sinai. The law cannot save. Nor can there be salvation by the overthrow of the law. Nor can there be salvation inconsistent with law. We may venture to say the problem is too deep for us. Humanity can neither save itself, nor see any way in which God himself can save the guilty.

Calvary furnishes the only solution. The probation under law is not final. The case is transferred from the law to the Gospel. Probation is carried over from the region of law to the provisions of grace. It is God who changed the venue and ordered the trial to proceed under new conditions. It is thus that salvation is of God.

I do not here enter the polemic as to how God could adjourn the case from strict justice or mere law to the court of mercy. It is sufficient that he did so do. That fact proves that it was in harmony with the eternal ethic of his nature to do it.

I re-affirm that it was a necessity to his nature to do so in his administration over a race and over the individuals of a race constituted as our race is. He could no more be an infinitely holy God without the mercy which provides a possible pardon to sin in a case such as man's, than he could if the principle of justice were left out of his administration. God's throne could not stand unimpeached under the single aspect of abstract and inexorable justice as the dominating principle of administration. I venture to go yet further, and to affirm that there is no such attribute in God as abstract justice unintoned with mercy. He is always just; never less than just; but he is also always merciful. It is a necessity to the peace of the universe that his throne should be clothed with the milder attribute of compassion in any degree that will be consistent with the general welfare of the system. Mere justice is the last resort of administration after mercy has exhausted all its resources. The final act of justice in awarding punishment can never be reached without previous efforts of mercy to avert the necessity; so that justice does not stand alone in the administration.

The seemingly contradictory ideas of rigorous justice and placable mercy are the immutable foundation of the ethical system. They are twin and mutually modifying attributes of the divine nature, never separated and, neither, never alone in administration. Together they constitute the holiness of the divine law and the eternal holiness of the divine nature as that nature is expressible in administration over finite beings. If it is possible to conceive of abstract justice as an element of the divine nature, it must be apart from administration. When the Infinite passes out of himself into relations with the finite, the eternal ethic of his own nature requires that his dealings with them should be mercifully tempered to their condition.

Invitation or vocation.—Following conviction and the despair which it awakens is the experience of a drawing of the spirit to God—a persuasion or invitation.

In the writings of the older and some of the recent Calvinistic theologians much is made of what they styled "vocation." It was placed as the initial experience of grace. The theory of election gave it its place and significance in the system. That theory, the supralapsarian form, was that antecedently to creation itself, indeed from eternity, God elected a certain definite number of souls yet to be created unto everlasting life—which number, and the particular souls included in it, was so fixed that it could neither be increased nor diminished—without any thought of any thing in them; and to secure the benefit of this sovereign and purely arbitrary election to them he gave his Son to make atonement for them and for them only, and his Holy Spirit to apply the saving benefits of the atonement to them in such manner that it should forever be impossible that any one of them should fail of salvation. Infralapsarians made the decree of election follow the lapse.

Vocation was declared to be the irresistible (sometimes modified in the use of other terms, as efficacious, effectual calling) grace whereby the Spirit caused elect souls to be willing to embrace proffered salvation. It was held that others were called; that is, invited; but the effectual call was only extended to the elect, and without the effectual call none could accept, but might reject, and be held guilty of the sin of rejection.

The doctrine of vocation as thus taught has no place in the word of God, and nothing analogous to it in Christian experience. The idea on which it rests is a defamation of God.

The only thing approaching it is the universal call of the Holy Spirit, which accompanies illumination and conviction, to all men to repent and turn to God. There is no foundation for the odious doctrine of a special effectual vocation to one and common vocation to another—the former addressed to elect souls and the latter to the non-elect.

It does accord with common experience that God calls upon all men every-where to repent, and by consequence that all men may respond—that is, that sufficient grace is extended to all to enable them to respond—to the invitation. To the illuminated and awakened soul the invitation is entreating and persuasive, —a divine drawing not because they are elect, but because they give heed. God never violates the eternal ethic of the spiritual world which applies to all spirits equally—that is, the law which forever treats them as free responsible persons, before whom he sets life and death, always and without discrimination offering life and making its attainment possible on the same terms and persuading them thereto. Any vocation that exists is a common, impartial, and universal vocation—never irresistible, always sincere.

The invitations are accompanied with the revelation of Christ as an atoning Saviour. The soul made conscious of the divine invitation, and having revealed to it that Christ is its Saviour and friend, through whom mercy may be obtained, and especially being informed of the sacrifice he made of himself for it, has begotten in it hope.

The fourth stage of experience is reached: penitence is begotten in the soul. The order cannot be reversed. There must be first illumination in order to conviction; further illumination in order to invitation, and invitation in order to hope, and hope in order to penitence.

If force were possible on ethical grounds there is every reason to believe it would be employed not in a few but in every case. It is excluded in an ethical system. Along with the invitation comes the further illumination that God will forgive. Christ is introduced as a Saviour.

As in order to conviction the soul must be brought face to face with broken law, so in order to hope of pardon, which is the dawn of repentance, it must be brought face to face with the Gospel—the invitations, promises, and mighty persuasions of love.

The repentance which ensues upon invitation and the opening to the soul of the door of a possible pardon is a well-defined experience, and its source is also well defined and its relation to precedent states natural and logical. It is impossible that it should exist without that which goes before.

We have said that it is a well-defined experience. It is proper that we should note what it is. The etymology of the term scarcely defines it. It does indeed imply or involve a retrospective thinking—a rethinking. In it the mind is carried back to the contemplation of its sin, and the thought of its sin is a second better thought; but it is more a feeling than a thought—a feeling begotten of a thought.

The first and natural effect of conviction, which is the state which immediately precedes repentance and which conditions it, is simple remorse and despair. These spring from the view the soul has of itself under law. They are the only feelings the soul can have under law.

Remorse and despair are not elements of repentance. In order to repentance the soul must be freed from these. While they possess it it is impossible any other emotion should enter; they paralyze every other feeling; their domination is death. Nor is repentance a mere barren regret which occupies itself merely, or even chiefly, with apprehended penal consequences of sin, or even the disgrace of sin. In this feeling, of mere regret as in despair and remorse, the soul is concerned only about itself. It is purely selfish; it has in it nothing redeeming or restorative; it is a sorrow that worketh death. All such states spring from the law which kills. They are of the essence of ultimate death of the soul—the gnawing of the worm that dieth not. In order to salvation the soul must be lifted out of them and delivered from them.

The first tendency under deep awakening of the soul to the sense of sin is to these states, and they would inevitably become fixed states did not the Holy Spirit through the Gospel turn the gaze of the awakened and alarmed soul away from itself to its Saviour. The law having performed its function, the Gospel must come with its healing balm. Calvary must take the place of Sinai; remorse must give way to contrition. It is the broken heart that pleads for forgiveness. Repentance is the triumph of love. No sinful soul ever was or ever can be saved until it has a vision of love upon the throne of the universe. It is love that breaks the stony heart; it is love that unseals the fountain of penitential tears; it is love that inspires the cry for forgiveness.

Repentance thus inspired by the revelation of love embraces these elements. It is a composite grace, the recognition of God as a loving, long-suffering, patient, and forgiving Father; it sees him in Christ on the cross for its redemption; it beholds him with extended arms calling to it, the father waiting the return of the prodigal child; it says, "I will arise and go to my father;" it says, I have nothing but sin; it feels its poverty and shame, its filthy rags and disgrace; it renounces all the past and turns its back upon it; it detests and hates its sin. Not daring to look up it wails its piteous lament, rushes into the father's arms, and sobs upon his bosom: "Father, I am no more worthy to be called thy son: make me as one of thy hired servants." This is repentance. No other feeling is genuine repentance.

The next point we make is that repentance is not an ultimate end as an experience. It conditions a further experience. If it were possible to conceive the experience to stop with it, it would be to no purpose. Appropriate as it manifestly is it would not be satisfactory as a fixed state. It is impossible to the mental or ethical nature to find content in it as an end. We are under the necessity of viewing it as means to an end.

The end for which it exists is forgiveness. The whole movement of the consecutive and correlated experiences from the start is to that end. Does it reach the end? No. Can the end be reached without it? No. Does it go toward the end? Yes. No soul smitten with sin can be forgiven without repentance. We pause at this point for a moment. The fact which we assert here with such positiveness, that a soul cannot be forgiven without repentance, is fundamental. It is not simply because God has made repentance a condition of forgiveness that forgiveness cannot take place without it. We do not say that a volitional condition might not be made the ground of pardon, but we do say that this is not one of that kind. There is an irreversible ethical reason why it is so.

This will appear if we consider what forgiveness means. The experience of forgiveness is not the next sequent upon repentance, and it will be stated in its proper place; but we briefly refer to it here. Forgiveness means restoration to favor. To suppose that it could take place without repentance would imply that an impenitent sinner—that is, a sinner in whose heart there is still the love and practice of sin—could be regarded with favor. The idea subverts the essential principle of ethics. Repentance is therefore a necessary antecedent to forgiveness.

But, then, has atonement in Christ no relation to pardon? We answer, Yes; it has every thing to do with it, so much so that there is no pardon without atonement. The atonement conditions all experience of salvation. Infants even are not saved without atonement. The heathen who never heard of Christ, nevertheless if saved at all, and we cannot doubt that many of them are saved and all might be, their salvation is conditioned by the atonement. The atonement conditions divine forgiveness in every case. Without atonement in Christ there is no salvation; but the atonement does not alone save. It provides a possible salvation, and under the Christian law the salvation which is made possible by atonement is conditioned on "repentance toward God and faith in Jesus Christ." There is no forgiveness under the Christian dispensation promised on any other ground.

Repentance itself is offspring of atonement. Atonement does not save without repentance, but it furnishes the conditions of repentance to the transgressor, and it furnishes the conditions of pardon on the part of the sovereign, and atonement arises self-moved in the divine heart. It is outbirth of God's love: "God so loved," etc. In order to properly understand the fact and significance of repentance, the relation of atonement to Christian experience and to salvation needs to be more fully explained. To attempt to explain the philosophy of Christian experience and salvation without the atonement is the same absurdity as to explain them without Christ. Not a single element of experience can be explained without Christ and without atonement in Christ.

The polemic touching the relation of atonement to pardon we cannot enter here at length or in further detail.

Let us keep constantly in mind that we are not simply aiming to give a true statement of the facts of Christian experience, but also a philosophy of it; that is, an explanation of the sources or conditioning grounds of the facts and their significance to an end—their coherence and unity.

We have found what repentance is, and we have found how it becomes an experience of the soul. We have seen that it is an incident in a line of incidents, which is in order to ultimate salvation; that is, the restoration of the soul to the forfeited favor of God and the enjoyment of his forgiving love. Is it not manifest that as an experience it occupies its precise and only possible place in the line of incidents? Could it change place with any preceding experience? Is it not conditioned upon antecedent sin and conviction of sin under law? Is it not conditioned further on illumination or revelation of the Gospel? Is it not precisely the experience which logically and ethically should follow these antecedent and conditioning experiences? Could the ultimate outcome ever be reached without it?

We now make the point that, while repentance is absolutely necessary to pardon, it is not the last necessity precedent. Were the experience to stop here pardon could not become an accomplished fact. It is difficult to conceive how a really penitent soul should not be forgiven. I venture the position that such a case does not exist; nevertheless, another act intervenes between penitence and pardon as final condition. That act is the act of faith.

It, after all, is the essential act. "Salvation is by faith." All that precedes faith is conditioning to it, as it is conditioning to salvation. Take away what goes before, faith becomes impossible. Leave out faith, salvation becomes impossible.

Repentance brings us to the point in the line of spiritual movement where faith becomes the natural and logical next. Up to this point we have these facts: the sinner slain by the law; the sinner under the illumination of the Gospel brought to repentance and supplicating for mercy. He has as yet received no assurance of pardon; in fact, he is not pardoned—the burden of the sense of guilt is still upon him.

Is there any thing more that he can do—anything else that he is required to do? If so, what is that next logical sequent? He has been moved by manifestations of love, and by invitations and promises, to repent and sue for pardon. Now, how can pardon become a realized fact in his consciousness? Manifestly it is impossible without a further act on his part. He must have faith—he must implicitly trust the promises. Faith is the hand by which he received the pardon. It cannot be bestowed, that is, it cannot reach him, without faith. Not only can he not be conscious of pardon without faith, but the fact of pardon cannot take place in the divine mind without faith in the recipient. Non-faith leaves the soul still in an attitude of unreconciliation—it is of the nature of sin.

You will observe that not only does faith become a necessity in order to the next fact which emerges in the moral movement, that is, pardon—the end for which the whole process exists—but it occupies the precise place it must occupy in the movement. It could not possibly exist antecedently to repentance. It is impossible that an impenitent soul should have faith. It must first repent before it can trust God for pardon. To trust him for pardon while it is in a state of impenitence is to blaspheme his holiness. Faith must respect immutable, ethical principles and conditions. When the soul is repentant faith is made possible to it, and therefore required of it on the two grounds of promise, and the intuition that penitence, if alone it does not furnish a condition which ethically demands pardon, does furnish a condition which seems to make pardon possible and proper. Given the atonement and attendant invitations and promises, together with the helpful influence of the Holy Spirit, and the intuition of an ethical propriety to support the mind, it makes the demand for faith not oppressive, but both reasonable and ethical—it ought to be.

Let us now inquire more critically, what is faith? We shall find in the analysis why it is that faith occupies so conspicuous a place in the scheme of salvation.

What is faith? We note, first, in answer to the question, What is faith? that faith is a free act of the soul by the soul. The Calvinistic fundamentum—for it is that to the system, that God creates faith in the soul, except in a modified sense—is false in fact; and in view of the place which it holds in the scheme of salvation it is unethical. Faith is a complex mental, emotional, and volitional act; the proper conditions of which are furnished to the soul, but it is the proper act of the soul itself. If salvation is by faith, and if faith were created in the soul by a sovereign act of God, we have as the inevitable outcome that salvation is a necessitated result; and along with it all the unethical inclusions of that fact. To make faith a condition of salvation, and then make God the author of faith, is to transfer the conditions from the subject soul and make God condition a result of his own act upon his own performance. Faith, while a free act, is an act which is under mental law, not a capricious act. There are conditions under which alone it can take place. The soul has no power to exercise faith unless the conditions of the faith act exist. An impenitent soul cannot exercise faith. To suppose that he can is to suppose the soul capable of believing that God can and will forgive sin while sin is rampant in the soul; and it is more than that: it is to suppose the soul able to commit itself to God trustingly while it is raging against him; it is a contradiction. Thus faith as a condition of salvation involves also penitence as a condition of salvation, and all the antecedents of penitence which condition it. This we emphasize as an important statement. It is sometimes said, salvation is by faith alone—naked faith. If it means that salvation is not without faith, or that salvation always ensues upon faith as final condition, the statement is correct; but if it means that the final faith act may stand alone and apart from precedent states and acts, so that salvation can be without them, it is not a correct statement; and it is ethically vicious, and dangerously misleading. Faith is placed as the condition of salvation as including all conditioning antecedents—atonement in Christ, conviction of sin, repentance, confession, and supplication. These concomitants, unitedly and never separately, furnish the ethics of pardon; that is, the ethical ground on which pardon can be and is issued.

We return to the inquiry, what is faith? We have said it is a composite intellectual, emotional, and volitional act; that is, it is an act in which the entire soul—intellect, sensibilities and will—is exercised; in which the entire soul surrenders itself to God as Lord and Sovereign, as well as Saviour. It is thus not an ephemeral or superficial phase of feeling, or thought, or belief merely; but a radical and fundamental act which determines the character and future course of the soul's life—an act in which the soul accepts pardon on God's terms.

If we analyze this act we shall find that it includes these elements—*belief, trust, commitment.* The intellectual element is *first* in order, and conditioning to the others. Faith begins with belief; *but* does not end with it. It is not mere belief. The terms are sometimes used interchangeably. As a philosophic technic, they are identical. As a Christian technic, belief is only an element of faith, but an essential element. The belief element in faith, most comprehensively, is belief in the mercifulness of God and his willingness to forgive sin. Without this there can be no movement of the soul toward God. This form of faith may, under the enlightening influence of the Holy Ghost, arise in a heathen soul, and under the same helpful influence may issue in salvation. But the belief element in Christian faith is more than this: it is belief in the mercifulness of God, and his willingness to forgive sin, and in Jesus Christ his only begotten Son as revealed in the Holy Scriptures. With this essence of truth in the belief there may coalesce more or less of error in all minds without so vitiating the belief as to destroy its essential value. One believes in the High-Trinitarian doctrine, another is tinctured with Sabellianism, another with Arianism, or semi-Arianism, or Unitarianism; one interprets according to Calvinism, another is Arminian. These are severally phases of intellectual and fallible interpretation; perhaps, or possibly—certainly none of them absolutely accurate; some of them mere logomachy—dispute about words. There may be in minds holding any of them a sufficient essence of faith to make it saving. Absolute orthodoxy can scarcely be made a condition of salvation. There is an essence of faith which may be enveloped in some error. This must be allowed, or among fallible beings the way of salvation, narrow enough, would be made perilously strait. While it may be perfectly clear that certain beliefs are of that essence, and that certain other beliefs exclude it, it is not for us to decide precisely what in all cases the exact form of belief must be. It is neither wise nor safe for one class of minds to attempt to impose its precise forms of thought upon all othess; or to make its precise formulas the standard by which eternal destinies are to be determined. It is sufficient to say that the belief element in faith is belief in the mercifulness of God and his willingness to forgive sin; and belcif in Jesus Christ as the Redeemer and Saviour of men. This element cannot be excluded from the faith which saves.

But no form of belief is saving faith. "The devils believe." Possibly among the devils we should find sounder orthodoxy as to matters of belief than among the most astute theologians. Who knows! The belief may be the most accurate possible, and yet the faith which saves be wanting. The belief element is an act of the mind, simply as mind determining what to it seems to be true. There is nothing ethical in it simply as belief. Belief acquires all of its importance as conditioning an ethical act—an act of the affection and will; and so affecting character and conduct. If it stop short at mere belief, it is not of the slightest ethical value.

We have said that faith is conditioned by repentance, and that faith to the impenitent is impossible. It is important to exact accuracy that we now say that the belief—element of faith in some degree antedates repentance and conditions it. Without belief in God and the immutable ethic of his law there could be no conviction of sin; and without belief in his mercifulness there could be no repentance. Thus faith, in the single aspect of belief, emerges in the whole process from the beginning to the end of Christian experience. It is in its final ethical form, as an act of the affection and the will, "called faith of the heart," that it is conditioned by repentance, and is made the condition of salvation.

We come now to consider what that final ethical form of faith is which is unto salvation. It is most generally called "heart trust." That phrase hardly adequately expresses it. It leaves out, or at least leaves in too great obscurity, the will element. In matters of mere belief neither the affections nor the will have any prominent place, if they have any place at all. The intellect merely is active. It is for this reason that the ethical element is absent. Mere belief is never matter of command, and never a ground of moral approbation as partaking of the nature of a virtue or grace. But in the final form of faith both the affections and the will are active. The soul profoundly moved in its sensibilities, moved and attracted by the love of God, moved with an affection such as a sinning child feels toward a grieved father, moved with contrition, deeply feeling its own grievous wrong and desiring forgiveness, sues for pardon. Upon the basis of these emotive states there arises trust. The faith act is completed by the soul, thus moved to trust, volitionally committing itself to God. It is an act of choice and free, and an utter self-determination to righteousness, in which the soul gives itself to God, and trusts him for forgiveness, and goes over and stands with him. It has in it the spirit of obedience—righteousness. The act rests upon the promises and that which underlies them, the great atonement of Christ, and the feeling inspired by the Holy Ghost, that it may commit itself to divine mercy for forgiveness.

LECTURE 6.

ELEMENTS OF CHRISTIAN EXPERIENCE—CONTINUED.

We have now completed the line of experience through which the soul passes antecedent to and conditioning of pardon. We have seen that they emerge in a rational order, each conditioning that which follows, in such manner that the order cannot be reversed or modified, both on mental and moral grounds. We have seen that they take their rise from the fact of sin; that they have for their end pardon. We have seen that such is the nature of God that no one of them could be left out and pardon be possible; that there is a strict harmony between them and the demands of an ethical system. We have seen also that they accord with the teaching of revelation and with the constitution of the spiritual universe.

The only question that remains to make a complete philosophy of them is, Are they adapted to the end of pardon; that is, do they furnish an adequate ground for pardon?

To this question we answer in three parts: First, if pardon is to be administered at all it must be on some conditions. If man is to furnish any of the conditions it is impossible to conceive of any others than those mentioned. There remains nothing more that he can do. Second, we answer: the conditions that will justify the pardoning act God alone can determine; and he has declared that upon these conditions he will administer pardon. Third, we answer: complying with these conditions, souls do experience pardon.

We add: if there is any salvation for the race at all, or any individuals of it, it must be through pardon, as, if penalty is not remitted, it must be executed. This is not an arbitrary, reversible, statutory arrangement, but a fundamental ethical necessity.

We add further: that it is impossible to conceive of any interests of the universe, including sovereign and subjects, suffering by the administration of pardon on the conditions placed.

We now enter upon the examination of another class of experiences. Those already examined were conditioning to salvation—or pardon, which is present salvation; conditions which the soul performs, and divine helps thereto. Those experiences upon which we now enter are experiences which arise together with and after the realization of salvation. Those were the experiences of a soul in its progress from a state of guilt and alienation to pardon. These are the experiences of a soul at the time and after it has come to God and has received pardon. In the former experiences man was more prominent; in these experiences now to be examined God is more prominent as actor; but throughout God and man are co-factors. In the former the prodigal is seen returning to his father; in these the father is seen receiving and reinstating the prodigal.

Our immediate work will be to state the experience the soul has on its initiation to life. Further on we shall deal with its experience after it has been initiated; along the way of its journeying until it is finally saved.

Pardon. Following the faith act, and conditioned by it on the human side and by the atonement on the divine side, are pardon, forgiveness, and regeneration. These three facts are concurrent, and unitedly constitute what is scripturally and theologically known as justification. But for a clear understanding it is necessary to consider these terms separately and so to ascertain the exact contents of each.

The terms pardon and forgiveness are so nearly synonymous that they are constantly used as identical. They are not, however, perfectly identical; but they are so cognate that when the difference is pointed out it is safe to use them interchangeably with the understanding that either term includes the other.

Pardon, in strictness and as used in the Scriptures, is an administrative act by which the penalty of sin affixed by law is remitted, not exacted.

Forgiveness is a personal act, which includes pardon, but goes further in that it not only includes the remission of penalty but reinstates the offender in the favor of the offended—restores loving relations between them. When pardon is understood in this broader sense, as it constantly is, there is no use for the added term forgiveness.

Under the divine government sin is not simply an offense against law, exposing the guilty to penalty, but it is an offense to God, awakening his personal displeasure against the culprit. His relations are personal as well as administrative. Pardon affects both his feeling and administration with respect to the offender when used in the broader sense of forgiveness. By forgiveness his displeasure is assuaged and his love restored, as well as penalty remitted. The pardoning act brings offender and offended into loving relations to each other. Under the divine government penalty is never remitted without forgiveness.

We have said that pardon, in its lowest sense, is the remission of penalty. Now let us pause to determine exactly what that means. A remitted penalty is a penalty deserved, but not inflicted. When the penalty is inflicted pardon is excluded. When pardon is extended the infliction of penalty is excluded. This is not a mere etymological or lexical demand of the terms. It is a strict and necessary ethical demand. A sin that is punished cannot be pardoned; and *vice versa*, a sin that is pardoned cannot be punished. The one term excludes the other. Now, if this is true, pardoned sin is never, and never can be, punished sin, and punished sin never is, and never can be, pardoned sin; or, more definitely still, sin cannot at the same time be both pardoned and punished, nor can it, under a holy administration, be neither pardoned nor punished, but must be one or the other. This statement is held to be axiomatic, and is postulated as such.

The effect of the foregoing postulate is to do away with the theological fiction of substitutional punishment which has been made to serve so important a part in the Calvinistic creed, and in the Arminian creed as well, by misinterpretation. The fiction is this, as placed in the Calvinistic creed: that by election of sovereign grace a certain number of souls were deeded by covenant to Christ, and that for these he made atonement, which atonement consisted in his taking upon himself the penalty of their sins—that is, received their punishment; in view of which they are graciously pardoned. The fiction involves the contradiction above named; namely, that the sins of the elect are both punished and pardoned. This itself is fatal to it, without taking account of its other unethical elements, which are numerous and some of them atrocious, but which our limits will not permit us to name even. The full discussion will be found in the volume on "Atonement in Christ" in *Studies in Theology*.

The theological fiction as it appears in some Arminian theorizing, while free from some of the most offensive inclusions of the Calvinistic creed, is not entirely free from the fault specifically mentioned here. The Arminian theory is often so stated as to involve the doctrine of substitutional punishment and becomes heir to all its embarrassments, among others the contradiction involved. It seems to be about this: that Christ took upon himself the punishment due the sins of the whole world and actually suffered it, the satisfaction to divine justice being full and complete; nevertheless, he does not release sinners themselves from the penalty unless certain conditions are complied with, but when the conditions are complied with the sins are pardoned. Now, here the same contradiction emerges as in the former case, the contradiction of the same sins being both pardoned and punished. It escapes the infamy of the doctrine of election, but it is heir to the other infamies of punishing the innocent for the guilty, and, worse even than Calvinism itself, the infamy of demanding conditions before the sinner shall be released from obligation to suffer the penalty which has already exhausted itself on a substitute, and, by consequence, liability to the re-infliction of the full penalty which has been once endured by another—worse than Calvinism.

The whole theory of substitutional punishment as a ground either of conditional or unconditional pardon is unethical, contradictory, and self-subversive.

Pardon is an administrative act, and as such always necessarily transpires in time. It is impossible that it should be an eternal act, that is, that it should exist from eternity. It always and necessarily implies the antecedent existence of the sin that is pardoned, and cannot be anticipative of it. Pardon of sins, therefore, at any given time, does not imply or include the pardon of sins that may occur subsequently, nor does it prevent the occurrence of subsequent sins. Sins subsequent to pardon need to be pardoned, or their penalty holds as if no preceding pardon for preceding sins had taken place. There is no escape from the penal consequences of any sin in any other way than through pardon.

Penalty is eternal if not remitted; that is, if pardon be not extended. The guilt of sin does not expire, by lapse of time, at the end of a given amount of penalty. Forgiveness is necessary to its termination. Once guilty, the soul must permanently remain guilty, unless forgiveness supervenes to remove the guilt. No amount of suffering can purge it. It cannot purge itself. The act which purges it must emanate from the being against whom it is committed. There is no end to its demerit except as forgiveness ends it. The penalty is death, and death is eternal, if not revoked.

Pardon is God's own administrative act, and must always be in accordance with his infinite holiness. Even God has no power either to withhold or administer pardon capriciously or arbitrarily or unethically, that is, to the infringement of the holiness of his nature.

Pardon is an act of the divine sovereign toward the sinning subject which releases the subject from the obligation to suffer the penalty due his sin and releases the sovereign from the obligation to inflict penalty. It is thus seen that the pardon act affects both the sovereign and the subject. The act involves the ethical character of the sovereign, and the state of the subject and his relations to law and administration. It is impossible that God should maintain his character of a just and holy, or even wise and merciful, sovereign, if he exercised the pardoning power or prerogative arbitrarily or without respect to conditions. That would be to abrogate law, or immorally, unethically, to override it. It would be an act of sovereignty which would unhinge the moral system. It is an absolute necessity that there should be conditions precedent and concurrent.

Nothing is more certain, therefore, than that God, as a holy sovereign, can neither remit penalty nor restore to favor without conditions which show that he is not indifferent to sin.

It is worth while to say further that while the pardon act must be conditioned, it must also, to be of any avail, be attended with a subjective change in the recipient. Mere sovereign forgiveness which left the sinner a sinner still would be of no benefit to the recipient, and would be ruinous to the character of the sovereign and to the interests of the universe.

How does pardon become matter of experience? Pardon, as we have seen, is an administrative and a personal act of God. How does pardon become matter of experience to man? It is impossible that the soul should be conscious of an act of God in the same way as it is conscious of its own acts or state. Consciousness cannot transcend the subject. It is strictly limited to subjective experience; but the pardoning act is not a subjective experience, but it is the act of another. How, then, can the fact of pardon become matter of experience? And what precisely is the experience?

To this question there can be but one answer: "The soul feels the assurance that it is pardoned." The feeling is its experience. The act of pardon transcends experience, but the feeling of pardon is matter of experience. The act God performs; the responsive assurance the soul feels. That there is a divine witnessing in the soul which produces the experience of assurance of the pardoning act is the testimony of God himself. With the forgiveness he creates the consciousness of it by causing the soul to feel the joy of it. The feeling of guilt is removed, and the feeling of pardon is imparted; but, as the act of pardon takes place in the divine mind, all the experience the soul can have of it is the feeling that it has been done, and the concomitant emotions attending it.

Concurrently with pardon and forgiveness, which, as we have seen, is an administrative act of God, releasing the soul from guilt, that is, the obligation to punishment, and releasing God from the obligation to inflict punishment; and restoring the soul to favor, an act witnessed to the soul by God himself, is a work done *in* the soul, generally designated by the term regeneration, and variously characterized in the Scriptures as "being born again," "created anew in Christ Jesus," "cleansed," "quickened," "renewed," and other descriptive phrases of similar import.

What is regeneration? Perhaps there is no subject-matter of experience about which there has been more confused thinking than that described by these terms. Uncritical and unscientific ignorance has woven a garb of sensuousness about them. Creed theologizers have added to the confusion. The imagination has been left to run wild and invest them with all sorts of meaning. Without doubt the case is one of real difficulty. On two points all agree: First, that regeneration is a work wrought in the soul; second, that God is the agent. There is disagreement on three points: First, as to the time-relation of the act to other parts of the experience, Calvinistic theologians placing it at the initiation, before faith and pardon, Arminians placing it subsequent to faith and concurrently with pardon; second, there is difference as to the question whether it is a conditioned act, or one wrought by pure sovereignty without conditions; third, there is difference as to precisely what is done. The first and second of these points are theological questions upon the polemics of which I cannot enlarge.

The third point is that which my thesis requires me to handle. The philosophy of the experience demands that the experience should be determined. I postulate that, as matter of experience, it is concurrent with pardon; is subsequent to faith and conditioned on the existence of faith—that it is synergistic and not monergistic.

To determine what regeneration is, it is necessary to recur to the subject of pardon. We have said that pardon is an administrative act of God which relates to the guilt of the soul, and which cancels guilt. Upon this point, I believe, there is perfect agreement.

Now, the first point I make is this: that pardon disposes of the question of guilt. If, with the Calvinist, we make guilt to include demerit for original sin, so called, as well as all personal sins, then pardon purges from the guilt both of original sin and of all personal sins. Or, if we take the Arminian view, that guilt is only predicable of personal sins, then pardon purges from the guilt of personal sins. In either case pardon disposes of the whole question of guilt. When sin is pardoned there is no remaining guilt. I attach great importance to this point, and therefore particularly emphasize it.

The next point I make is this: if pardon is an administrative act, which finally and completely disposes of guilt, then regeneration has nothing to do with guilt. It does not at all deal with the question of guilt or in any way refer to it—pardon has extinguished it; it is *non est*.

What, then, is the function of regeneration?

We make the point that regeneration has to do with the soul itself—the condition and state of its powers. All the terms descriptive of it are in harmony with this.

The consideration of this point will raise two inquiries: First, What is the condition of the soul prior to regeneration? Second, What is effected by regeneration?

On the first point, "What is the condition of the soul prior to regeneration?" we affirm in general terms that it is not in a normal condition—is not as it was originally constituted. This abnormalcy, we affirm, is not peculiar to some souls, but is common to all souls; includes the entire race.

The original constitution of the soul, as has been shown, was that it was invested with double relations, one to the sensuous, the other to the supersensuous, or spiritual world. The equation of its powers was such that it was able to decide for itself whether it would determine itself to the sensuous or supersensuous. Its law was that it should determine itself to the spiritual; that is, that the spiritual should dominate; that in all things the sensuous life should be subject to the spiritual—should be governed and regulated by it. Its righteousness was made to depend upon its self-determined, that is, its free conformity to this divine constitution. The statute under which it was placed recognized, and was based upon, this divine constitution, and served as a test whether it would conform to it; that is, whether the spiritual or sensuous should dominate it—whether the animal or divine should have the rule.

The free soul revolutionized itself—renounced the order established for it; put the reins of government in the hands of the sensuous and reduced the spirit to subjection; put the beast upon the throne, and made the angel serve in chains.

This was an act of rebellion and involved guilt. These results followed: (1) God's favor was lost—guilt always and necessarily involves that; (2) the helpfulness of his love and approving presence with the soul was withdrawn. (3) The equation of the soul's powers was lost. The divine constitution under which it was created was shattered. The will and the affections were enslaved and bound to the sensual. The soul was marred, and self-determined to abnormalcy.

You will observe that even in this case abnormalcy was effect of guilt, not ground of it; not itself guilt but a condition of the soul superinduced by sin—and a condition from which it can never recover itself, and from which it can never be recovered while guilt exists, or until guilt is removed.

Now I affirm that this effect of abnormalcy which resulted from Adam's sin, and which consisted in the loss of the equation of his powers whereby he was able to determine himself to righteousness, and which sensualized his entire nature, descends by heredity to his posterity. The *effect*, observe. Abnormalcy of soul is a disease which taints us all—a moral leprosy. When we reach moral consciousness sensuality is found already regnant in our affections and will by heredity.

Does it involve us in guilt? I affirm, no; it is ethically impossible. It is impossible there should be guilt where there has been no action of the subject. Therefore I affirm that it is a case which the administrative act of pardon does not reach at all.

The point I now make is this: the pardon, which as we have seen is an administrative act, by which the soul is entirely purged of guilt, does not at all affect the abnormalcy of nature into which the soul had fallen and which has acquired additional strength by indulgence. But, then, what advantage could pardon be to it if it were still left under the dominion of sensuality—spiritually dead? None whatever.

This question points exactly to our remaining want, for which regeneration provides, and so indicates the function of regeneration and also determines what it is.

Concurrently with pardon, God, in the person of the Holy Ghost, returns to and takes up his loving and helpful abode in the soul from which guilt expelled him, and by his presence and agency he restores the lost equation—enables the soul to righteousness, rebuilds the shattered constitution, reduces usurpers to subjection, and reinstates the rightful sovereign. This is regeneration. The soul by the act is made normal. Sensuosity is not destroyed, for it belonged to the original constitution of the soul, but it is put in subjection. It is not necessary to assume that the reconstruction replaces the soul in its original condition. That is certainly not true, and it is impossible it should be true. It is a soul that has had a taste of sin; that is habited to the long-undisputed dominion of sense; that is still sphered in environments of evil; that is dwarfed in its faculties; whose lusts by indulgence have grown masterful. It is impossible to change these facts. The evil effects are not and cannot be eradicated by any agency at once. But this is what has happened: God has so revealed himself to the soul, and in the soul, that its long-alienated and debauched affections now return to him, and its weakened and wayward will has been empowered to give in its allegiance to him. The lost equation of its powers is restored.

This is not a dry, arid change. It is a spring in the desert; it is the shout of freedom when the gyves and chains are broken; it is life from the dead; it is the dawn of heaven in the dungeon of a despairing soul—the bridegroom, with his glorious train, lighting up the long-deserted chambers of his future home.

How is regeneration effected? The general answer to this question is not difficult. It is by the operation of the Holy Spirit in the soul of man conditioned by the posture of the soul. I emphasize conditioned by the posture of the soul. An impenitent soul cannot be regenerated. The effect, therefore, is not wholly monergistic. God works regeneration only when the soul is in condition to be the recipient. This fact determines the position which regeneration holds in the line of experiences by which the soul becomes Christian. It is the last in the line. Its conditioning antecedents are in a fixed order: conviction of sin, repentance, faith, forgiveness; the last in the line—that is, forgiveness—being concurrent with but logically precedent to regeneration. This invariable order is significant. It points to a law of sequence, each part having a relation to every other part determined by the constitution of the mind and fundamental ethics of the divine administration—the laws of the spiritual world.

How under these fundamental laws the Spirit operates regeneration in the soul is not given to us to know. The effect is a reconstruction of the soul—a re-adjustment of the reigning powers in it—a reversal of what by sin had become the dominant law of its life. Is the revolution effected by a direct act of the divine will, a direct energizing, or by instrumentality of truth divinely communicated? Probably both. We do know that truth is a mighty instrument for accomplishing spiritual results. We do know that the word of God is embodied power of God, that he communicates his saving energy through the word; but we do not know but that in regenerating the soul there is also a direct energizing in the intellect, the affections, and the will—a lifting, inspiring, recreative energy. The effect produced points to such immediate agency, and we see not how to account for it in any other way.

The state arrived at by the line of experiences which culminate in regeneration is called in the Bible, and in theological writings, justification. If I were set to write a theological disquisition it would be necessary that I should enter a wide field of polemics here; but this is not what my thesis demands. My work is to deal simply with an experience.

Does the term justification represent any thing in actual experience beyond what emerges in pardon and regeneration? We think, no. It is a biblical and theological technic which describes, not an experience beyond or different from forgiveness and regeneration, but how God views the forgiven and regenerate soul and what will be his treatment of it. In general terms it signifies that a forgiven and regenerated soul stands in the divine thought and feeling, and will be treated as if it had never sinned, as if its righteousness had never been fractured. Possibly the deepest analysis of Christian consciousness would discover an experience precisely answering to that fact; but, if so, it would be found to run so close to the consciousness of pardon and the feeling of adoption as to be scarcely differentiable.

In fact the state reached is fitly described by the term justification as describing how the forgiven soul stands related to God. The term forgiveness and the experience of forgiveness implies all that; but we cannot further enter the theological polemic.

Is the forgiven soul and the regenerate soul thereby made actually righteous? Here, again, opens a wide polemic upon which we cannot enter at large. One answers yes; it is righteous, that is, its faith is counted for righteousness. Another answers yes; it is righteous, but not in itself. It is made righteous by having Christ's righteousness imputed to it. I answer, if righteousness means absolutely purged of guilt, then the pardoned soul is righteous—for pardon removes guilt. If, more than that, righteousness means a determination of the affections and the will to righteousness, a fixed desire to be righteous, and a ruling purpose of the mind to be righteous, and a state in which the soul does not of knowledge and intent commit sin, then again yes. But if righteousness means flawlessness of act as compared with a perfect law, or absolute perfection as to nature, then, no.

God himself designates all forgiven and saved souls as rightcous. The righteousness of any man can only be relative. Only the infinite is absolutely righteous. Righteousness to any finite being means loyalty of the will to what is known or believed to be right—it is the spirit of righteousness. This God inspires in every truly regenerate heart. In its deepest import it is the righteousness of faith. Forgiven men, regenerated by the Holy Ghost, are judged and justified by their faith and by the works of faith. No faith is or can be counted for righteousness which contains not in it the spirit of righteousness—that is, which does not determine the soul to the obedience of the law of righteousness and brings not forth the fruits of righteousness.

There could be no greater mistake than to suppose that the justification which is by faith is the justification of a soul in which the spirit of righteousness is not implanted, or that God accounts a soul righteous either on account of faith or on account of the imputation to it of the righteousness of another, when in itself there is found the spirit of unrighteousness. That which is matter of experience to the soul in its justification is that it loves righteousness and loyally purposes as nearly as possible to fulfill all righteousness. Such a soul God accounts just, and will deal with it as if it had never sinned when he comes to judge it at the last day.

The justification which is concomitant with forgiveness and regeneration means not some unethical declaration of a righteousness which does not exist, but the acknowledgment of that which does exist but which the soul has obtained through faith. The precise facts in the case are these: the soul was an unrighteous soul; when it becomes justified it does not mean that it is justified in its former unrighteousness—declared righteous when it is not righteous—for any reason, for there could be no reason in such a contradiction. But it means this, rather: that it has been purged of its unrighteousness by forgiveness and has been made righteous by regeneration; and this was brought about by a series of experiences, the last of which was regeneration made possible by the atonement through faith. Therefore by faith it is treated as righteous—its past unrighteousness being blotted out, and its will being brought under the law of righteousness.

When it is said that faith is imputed for righteousness it cannot be meant that the soul is void of righteousness, and that faith answers to all the obligations of righteousness; but it means this, rather: that faith which unites the soul to Christ, securing forgiveness for past sin, secures also the allegiance of the soul to him which is actual righteousness. The righteousness inwrought is through faith; but it is a real principle of righteousness, by which the soul becomes righteous. When it is said that the soul is righteous in Christ's righteousness it is not to be understood that Christ's righteousness is made over to us, so that, unrighteous in ourselves, we are made righteous in his righteousness; but this, rather: our righteousness is derived from Christ in that it is through him that we attain unto it.

When the soul has been forgiven it is purged of past sin. By forgiveness its guilt is removed—it has ceased to be guilty; that is negative righteousness. When the soul is regenerated — that is, born of God—not only is sin removed, but the principle of righteousness is implanted in it; that is positive righteousness. By the conjoint process the soul is made righteous.

The regenerate soul is adopted of God. This is matter of experience. As in the case of pardon, adoption is a divine act. God puts the forgiven and regenerate soul among his children and constitutes it a child and an heir. The experience of the soul is a consciousness of affiliation—a home feeling in the household of faith. There is no more pronounced fact of experience than this. The *Abba*-father is put in the heart of the new-born child. The affiliated soul spontaneously utters it—feels it—knows itself no longer to be an alien and stranger, but a child. Whatever its past sin, however consciously unworthy, the sense of kinship now thrills it. It is at home under the family roof-tree. It has left its swineherd life and rags, and wears the family insignia. It sits at the family table and shares in the family joy. This is a strange fact. But yesterday this soul was an alien and outcast. It knew of God only as a name; possibly it doubted his existence; it thought of him even with dismay; it wanted nothing to do with him; if it could it would have annihilated him; his terrors made it afraid; it ran from his approach; its greatest dread was the idea that some day it would have to meet him; it detested the family name! Who can explain it? To-day it rushes to his arms; thrills with the mention of his name; longs for him "as they that watch for the morning." Now it is no longer an alien and stranger from God; but it is a *pilgrim* and *stranger* on the earth. That which was its only home is now no home for it. Heavenly attractions have caught it and heavenly voices call it. Again I say there is no more pronounced experience than this; and there is no accounting for it but on the theory that God has put himself into loving relations with the soul and created in it a feeling of affiliation.

All these several facts are facts attested in its consciousness by the Holy Spirit—the renewing and regenerating agent. It is a great and radical experience, and it carries with it so long as the soul is loyal to it—that is, so long as it remains a fact—the absolute and perfect title to eternal life, and guarantees the accomplishment of whatever further experience is necessary to bring it to the final possession of the eternal life to which by its adoption it has become heir. While it remains there is no flaw in the title and nothing can improve the title. This I assert with great and confident emphasis. The foregoing discussions we think clearly point out the process through which the soul passes in becoming Christian, and indicate the grounds and significance of each successive stage of the process. They show that to become Christian there is a genuine subjective experience. They clearly show God's method in saving men. They show what salvation is—that is, that it is deliverance from the incurred penalties of sin; but, more radically than that, that it is a subjective change wrought in the character of the soul itself, in the absence of which salvation in the inferior sense is impossible. They point out a sufficient reason for the whole process and each distinct stage of it. They show the relations of parts of the experience. They demonstrate that the entire process is strictly ethical, and in no respect artificial, mechanical, or whimsical, or arbitrary—that they are radical, and lie at the roots of the ethical well-being of the universe. They are consistent with righteousness in both of its essential parts—eternal justice and eternal love.

LECTURE VII.
SOME PHASES OF EXPERIENCE SUBSEQUENT TO REGENERATION.

We have seen in the lectures preceding God's method in recovering the soul of man from a state of guilt to a state of righteousness; it remains that we consider his further methods with it, preparatory to its admission to the everlasting blessedness to which, by its recovery from guilt and re-creation in righteousness, it has become heir *prospective*.

We attach importance to the phrase "*heir prospective*." By it we do not mean simply an heir whose accession to the inheritance is in the future, but an heir whose final accession to the inheritance is still further conditioned; an heir who has obtained a title if he do not forfeit it by future unfaithfulness, but a title which may be forfeited.

This leads to the further statement, that nothing experienced by the soul in its forgiveness and regeneration guarantees its final attainment to everlasting life. The doctrine of final perseverance is an unethical fiction. Probation does not terminate with regeneration; or rather regeneration does not terminate probation. We do not here enter upon the polemics of this statement, but proceed upon the *postulatum*.

The object of continued probation may be stated as triplex; first, still further to test the soul by subjecting it to trial and temptation that it may furnish the proof that its determination to righteousness is final—one which it will not reverse under any exigencies of its existence; and that, by the trial, the graces implanted in its regenerate life may have opportunity to grow in strength and beauty until they come to ripeness, robustness of manhood stature. No trial—no strength.

The second object of continued probation is that the regenerate soul may have opportunity to witness to the power of the grace of God to save from sin, and to keep the soul under all stress of trial and temptation in peace and assurance of faith; a witness not with the tongue *only*, or *chiefly*, but by a life well ordered and redolent of divine virtues; that it may shine as a light in the surrounding darkness of sin and unrighteousness, and by its shining light up the path to other pilgrims.

The third object of continued probation is that it may have the opportunity to become a co-worker with Christ—suffering and sacrificing with him, and devoting its life in all active and earnest labors for the world's salvation to which he devoted his life, even unto death.

All of which is summed up in the general statement that the object of continued probation is that the soul may attain to fixedness of character by its own free choice; that it may be perfected and forever established in holiness; that, rooted and grounded in faith, which is another name for loyalty, it may be prepared for all the unknown incidents and exigencies of its immortal existence, and be thoroughly fitted for "the inheritance of the saints in light"—the eternal companionship of God and the participation of his glory.

The further experiences of the soul after regeneration must be interpreted from the ends here indicated, and the philosophy of them will be found in their adaptation to the ends which they serve.

It is pefectly obvious that the objects proposed by prolonged probation are such as are vital to the soul itself, and such as are vital to the interests of the kingdom of God upon the earth. The soul itself needs the prolonged probation and cannot be brought to its final destiny without it; and the divine kingdom needs it and cannot be built without it. It is conceivable that a soul just purged of guilt and regenerated by the Holy Ghost might be instantaneously transferred to heaven, and it is not impossible that instances of the kind have occurred, but it is not God's ordinary method of procedure, and for the reasons above named.

Were it the ordinary method there could be no Church of God upon earth, and the means of carrying forward the divine kingdom, so far as is apparent, could not exist. God employs not merely the atonement, and the gospel of salvation and the agency of the Holy Ghost, but also regenerated men, in the salvation of men. Were it his method to remove regenerate men immediately on their regeneration there would then be no salt in the earth—there would be no regenerate men to remove.

Being men, it is impossible that they should be left here among men and not themselves be still on probation. Thus the divine economy with relation to the race involves probation prolonged, for a period longer or shorter as seen best by infinite wisdom and grace, after the grace of life has been imparted to the soul. These facts explain the divine economy for the continued probation of Christian souls. Of the fact there is no question. The existence of Christians on the earth is proof of it.

It is implied in the statement above that souls are not perfected in receiving the grace of forgiveness and regeneration; that, great as are the benefits bestowed in that experience, there are still remaining experiences to be wrought out in it during its prolonged probation, as well as ends to be accomplished by it. This is a point around which much needless confusion has grown. It needs careful statement.

Keeping in mind the fact that we are not essaying a theological or creed statement of Christian experience, but simply a statement of the facts, and a rational explanation of them, as of any other spiritual phenomena, we are ready to proceed.

Our present inquiry is as to the phenomena which emerge in experience, during prolonged probation, subsequent to the implanting of the divine life in the soul. It will help us in our further inquiries if we cast about for a moment to determine the exact status we have reached. This will furnish the data for further progress.

We have before us by supposition a human soul that has just become the recipient of forgiveness and the implanting in it of the divine life by the Holy Ghost. In preceding investigations we traced the process by which the soul was brought into its present state, and determined the meaning of the terms forgiveness and regeneration, which describe its present state. It is not necessary that we refer to these matters again. Our present inquiry has to do with the circumstances in which it finds itself now placed. The circumstances will be influential in determining its future experience, and must be noted in order to explain them.

The general fact is, that though the soul has been, by its recent experience, naturalized in the divine kingdom, so as to become a citizen and prospective heir of all the emoluments of citizenship, it is not yet in heaven.

The particular facts are: First, it is the same soul it was prior to its naturalization. It is important that we should emphasize this. It is not another soul. Nothing has been added to its prior self-essence, and nothing has been removed from its prior self-essence. All its old faculties and susceptibilities remain and no new ones have been added. In these respects it does not differ from its former self. The change that has taken place in it is simply a change as to the objects of its affections and the determinations of its will. These changes change its ethical quality and its relations. In these respects and in no other it is a new soul. The change is a radical change—a complete revolution; but it is one of ethical quality and relations, not of substance. It is the same soul that carries itself over into the new experience. There is an identity of the soul which holds from the dawn of existence to utmost immortality. There is an ethical quality of the soul determined by its voluntary relations to its law, which may vary from deepest guilt of sin to highest perfection of holiness, and which may at any time during probation change, either in degree or radically. This soul standing before us as just forgiven and regenerated has become ethically different from its former self—transformed. To prevent misapprehension of the phrase, "There is an ethical quality of the soul determined by its volitional relations to its law, which may vary from deepest guilt to highest holiness," I add that the soul cannot by mere volition change itself from a quality of guilt to a quality of holiness, though it may change itself from a quality of holiness to a quality of guilt. Only God can purge the soul of guilt; only God can implant holiness; but God can do neither of these without the free coaction of the human will; and that which gives ethical quality to the soul is found in its own act of will. We do not enter upon the polemic involved. The point we desire to hold distinctly before your minds is this: That the soul newly forgiven and regenerated is the identical soul that, prior to that, was guilty, and dead in trespasses and in sins.

It ought to be added that it is not only the same soul, delivered from former guilt, with a new ideal born within it and a new principle of life implanted—that is, a new governing motive and a new energizing toward righteousness—but, further, that it is a soul open to the same influences of evil which formerly prevailed with it and, additionally, still affected by the power of early dominant habit of evil. These are undoubted facts; and must be taken note of in accounting for its future experiences. But yet, more than that, it must be taken into the account that it is a soul whose knowledge is limited; whose intelligence is small; whose natural temper is irascible; whose will is weak; whose conscience is often warped by error—simply the soul of a man of common mold—not the spirit of an angel.

It should still be further added that it is a soul that has been maimed by sin; whose tone has been lowered by familiarity with vice; many times a soul that has been the prey of unbridled appetites and debauched by gross immoralities, until its conscience has become clouded and its ethical ideas confused; in which long-continued habits of evil—evils of thought, evils of desire, evils of feeling, evils of practice—have had undisputed sway. Who can measure the power of habit? Who can measure the power of indulged appetite? Stronger than withes and gyves of iron. To understand the after history of this soul into which a new constructive life has been introduced all these things must be taken into the account. They cannot fail to affect and color its future experience. The new constructive life has to contend with all these subjective conditions. It must meet and master these mighty forces. It must reduce this anarchy to order. Out of these ruins of sin it must rear a shapely temple of righteousness.

I note yet further that in this newly regenerate soul there is still remaining a life toward the flesh and toward the world.

The new life that has come to it has not wholly destroyed its old life, and never will while it remains in the body and on earth. The old life of sin has been removed and the new life of righteousness has been implanted; but the soul has a life toward the flesh and toward the world which is of its original constitution, and is in no sense sinful in itself. Whatever belongs to the original constitution of the soul is of divine origin and accords with the divine will. It is abuse which constitutes sin. Any abnormalcy which results from sin creates a demand for cure. The tendencies to the flesh and the world in the unregenerate soul are excessive and unregulated and dominant, and show soul-depravity. The new-born regenerate life does not remove the tendency, but regulates it and brings it under the law of righteousness.

Once more, and more explicitly, this regenerate soul is still a temptable soul; with the perilous power to yield to temptation. Every avenue of evil is left open to it. Every power of evil may assail it. Any moment it may yield.

There is another point which I think it important to mention here; it is this: any ethical state of any finite being undergoing probation is for the present moment only. The state of justification, or, as Bushnell very properly calls it, the righteousing, upon which a soul enters by forgiveness and regeneration, is momentary, and if it abides it must be moment by moment. This arises from the fact that we ourselves exist moment by moment, and never are except as we are in the passing moment. Our righteousness, therefore, must be re-affirmed every moment. As our righteousness is by faith at first, so it continues to be by faith. For our righteousness to abide faith must be a continuous act. It is for this reason that the righteous are said to live by faith. Faith is the well spring of their righteousness; cut off the fountain and the stream dries up. We are not made righteous once for all, but we must be renewed in righteousness continuously.

This I affirm, and deem it an important point. The ethical and spiritual state of any soul is not determined by what it was, but by what it is at the sharper than a needle point called "now." If maintained, and carried forward, it must be by consecutive re-affirmation both on God's part and the soul's part. There is and can be no necessary connection between the past and the present, or between the present and the to-morrow of the soul's ethical state. The soul carries its own existence through all the passing nows, and each now will come into the judgment. Pardon in any now carries with it pardon for every antecedent now. If from any moment when it is pardoned the soul remains *absolutely* loyal, and its faith be *constant* and *perfect*, from that moment it is a sinless soul, each now from the moment of pardon having been without sin. But this is an experience to which, it is safe to affirm, but few souls of men ever attain in this life.

The second fact I deem it important to note, in order to the explanation of subsequent experiences, is, the soul, new-born, is left to reside in its *old* body unchanged. There is not a particle of change effected in the body by the regeneration of the soul. All the change is wrought in the soul itself. No ethical quality is predicable of the body or any thing that the body does or feels. The ethic is in the soul, but the ethic of the soul is in many ways affected by its relations to the body. The body must be taken into the account in explaining spiritual experiences, and it is not, therefore, without significance that the soul, after regeneration, is left with its old companion, the body, unchanged. The state of the body affects the state of the soul.

The third point I note is this: the soul after its regeneration is left in the same world in which it lived before. By the same world we do not mean simply the same earthly habitation, but the same environments of all kinds. It is not separated, and cannot be, from men and institutions and pursuits which pertain to the earth, or from the contact and natural power of association, example, prevalent ideas, and practices of its fellows. It is left here to live the common life of humanity. To escape the contact of evil, it is not permitted to retire from the world and live the life of a recluse or hermit. No provision of this kind is made for the protection of its new born sanctity. It must go down into the arena and fight with the beasts. Not even the devils are kept aloof from it.

The fourth point I note is, this new-born soul, at the threshold of its new life, is beleaguered by malign and hostile forces interested to destroy its new life—to strangle it in its birth. It has not simply to encounter the difficulty of reconstructing character under the adverse influences of its own subjective evil habits and those which spring from the physical nature in which it is incarcerated, and from the current of the world, which sets against it, but must contend with organized powers of evil combined against all righteousness. I do not enter the polemic of a personal devil, or of Milton's dream of mighty hosts "who throng the air and darken heaven." Let those who can doubt. Whether or not there are unincarnate emissaries of evil, none can question that there is an incarnate kingdom of evil, intent on the ruin of souls and scheming the destruction of all righteousness.

I note, as a fifth fact, that the regenerate soul is still held strictly under the law of righteousness. The grace which, through the atonement and by faith, has secured to it forgiveness for sins that are past does not modify or change its relations to immutable ethical law. There is no place for antinomianism in the scheme of human salvation. To its utmost demand the law is forever binding upon the forgiven as much as upon the unforgiven soul. The pardon act is retrospective and is not a release from obligation for the future. I emphasize this fact also, as one of great importance, and which must be taken into the account in rendering a philosophy of the experience in prolonged probation of a regenerated soul. The new filial relation that has come to it does not release it from or in any way diminish its obligations to the law of righteousness. That law holds over it with unabated force. It must do the will of God, resisting all evil and fulfilling all righteousness. Nothing either in the provisions of the atonement or in its forgiveness of past sins removes from it an iota of its obligations to this law. It is matter of experience that every regenerate soul feels this obligation. It is an ethical necessity that it should be so; otherwise the atonement, which was made for life, would work death, and forgiveness and regeneration would work all manner of unrighteousness. It is impossible that any thing God does for the soul should emancipate it from the obligations of righteousness without introducing anarchy into the moral system. He may, as we have seen, on conditions which conserve righteousness, forgive, and only on such conditions; but he has no power to release a moral being from the obligation without himself thereby becoming the patron of unrighteousness, and so vitiating his own holiness. Every spirit in the universe must forever be answerable to that law, and the throne of eternal holiness must forever preserve and enforce that law in full and unabated vigor. The safety of the moral system depends on this principle. Sap it and the moral system falls into anarchy. The law of God marks out a narrow path, and the grace of God does not widen it.

The sixth fact which I deem it important to state is, there is a divine kingdom, organized of God, established in the earth, and composed of regenerate souls. Of this kingdom, by its regeneration, the new-born soul has now become a member. It has its duties, its helps, and its fellowships—all of which are for him. It has its Bible for his guide, its God-ordained minister for his instruction and shepherding, its Sabbath for his rest and worship, its sacraments for his observance, its appointed services for his comfort and upbuilding in faith, its fellowship meetings for mutual prayer and experience, its organized plans of Christian work for his sympathy and co-operation. It is his spiritual home; the birthplace of his soul. Its members are his brothers and sisters. Wherever he goes in all the earth this household of faith has an open door for him. But it does not exist for his delectation alone. It has no provision for drones. It opens opportunity for useful work to each of its members and imposes obligations upon them. It demands purity, loyalty, earnestness, and dilligence.

It is manifest that the manner in which this new-born soul shall deport itself in the house of God, the use it shall make of it, its improvement of its privileges, its fidelity to its obligations, will determine what its experience will be.

I notice a further and final fact, going into the status reached by regeneration, which must be taken into the account in explaining the future experiences of this just-forgiven and regenerated soul; that further fact is, it is a soul in which God has not only wrought a work, but in which God is deeply interested, and in which he has taken up his residence. It is not a soul left to itself to fight its own battles. Its implanted life is divine. Were it dissevered from its source it would perish in a day. All the powers of righteousness are in God and from God. Separated from the fountain, it is safe to say, no angel could stand, much less the soul of man, weakened in all its powers and beleaguered with evil. We emphasize it, therefore, as matter of importance to be taken into the account, that God is *with* and *in* his new-born child, and all his almighty power is guaranteed for his support, if he will.

We attach importance to the phrase, *if he will*. It is a free soul, which, while it has no power, left to itself, to overcome evil, has power to avail itself of Almighty power or to dissever itself. But that which I wish to emphasize is that it has God with it, and may command his help at any moment. This is its refuge, into which it may run and hide, and within whose cover it is safe. This, I affirm, is matter of experience, not mere doctrine or theory. It pertains to the philosophy of probationary history that it should be recognized. Without it no soul could escape from the dominion of sin, and work its way through an earthly life to everlasting blessedness. Without it there could be no justification of God in placing man in his earthly environments. Without it probation would be an empty name—a tragedy of farce.

Now, with these facts before us we are prepared to consider the further experiences of a regenerate soul. These facts are so conditionary that they imply very much what the experiences will be. Our business is to inquire what they are, what they possibly may be, and what they ought to be.

It will aid in the examination of these points if we can place distinctly before our minds an ideally perfect standard to which to compare attainments. The standard *is* the ideally perfect. The aim of grace is to raise the soul as nearly as possible to the realization of the ideal. The demand on the regenerate soul is that it endeavor constantly after the nearest approximation possible to it. Of these three points we think there can be no doubt.

The difference between the actual state of the soul's experience and the state possible to be attained or to have been attained will point out the defects of experience or state of the soul which will demand improvement. The possible is required, and only the possible. Defect, as compared with the possible, not with the ideal, is moral defect, and demands improvement.

Now, what is the ideal standard for a finite soul posited as man is? The standard in God is absolute—changeless and infinite ethical perfection. That is not the standard for any created being, because to such perfection the finite can make no approach. That can be no standard which cannot be approached.

The ideal of a perfect man. Man is a soul. The experience is, therefore, that of a soul comprising intellect, sensibilities, and will—sensibilities including the entire emotive nature, desires, affections, sensitivities passions, and appetites. An ethically perfect soul is one which perfectly knows its law and perfectly obeys it—a soul whose intellect unerringly discerns between things which ought to be and those which ought not to be; a soul delicately sensitive to slightest approach of evil or wrong; a soul whose affections are so regulated that only those things are loved which ought to be loved and whose desires do not covet things that are discerned to be wrong; a soul that supremely loves God and revolts at whatever would displease him; a soul rightly affected toward the welfare of all other sentient existence and loving other souls as it loves itself; a soul whose will is unfalteringly determined to all righteousness and against all unrighteousness; a soul that with eager delight chooses both to do and suffer all that it ought to do and suffer and promptly refuses to do every thing that it ought not to do every moment of its existence, with perfect freedom and with full consciousness of power to the opposite and in the presence of all possible temptations to the opposite.

It is perfectly obvious that this ideal has never been reached by any but one man on the earth. It was reached by Jesus of Nazareth. This fact places him forever unapproachably out of the category of merely human souls. It is also perfectly obvious that if ultimate salvation depended upon the realization of this ideal no child of man could ever be saved. It follows that the impossible ideal is not what is required by the eternal ethical law. That which is required of the human soul is the nearest approach possible. That is required, and any failure marks not only defect but in some sense culpable defect, which, to free us from its consequences, will require the continuous compassionate treatment which infirmity must always lay under tribute.

The standard of privilege and of duty laid upon the soul, if not to reach this ideal of a perfect man, because for some reason it is impossible, is that the soul should make the utmost effort to do so—is that it should approach it as nearly as possible; possible not to itself alone by its own unaided power, but as nearly as possible with all available helps at its command. This is the ethical law that is binding, and comparison with which determines the degree of its moral perfection or imperfection—approvableness or unapprovableness to God.

Now, with this standard of ideal perfection and with this standard of duty, let us proceed to determine what are the actual facts of Christian experience. We desire as nearly as possible in the statement which follows to be true to facts without prejudice or partiality. The object is to describe Christians as they show themselves; as we, being one of them, have known them for sixty years. Two extremes must be avoided—the extremes of under and of overestimating them. There is such a correlation between subjective states and external manifestation that the latter is a fair interpreter of the former. A man is generally internally approximately what he habitually shows externally. The tree is, and must be, judged by its fruits. The law of interpretation applies to all, and as it is a test furnished by our Lord we may not shrink from it.

Taking this rule, we affirm that there is a radical difference between Christian and unchristian souls. Unsatisfactory as the account we must give of ourselves may be, it will nevertheless show that fact. There is a regenerate family on the earth, and it shows its divine lineaments, though often sadly blurred; but the faults of Christians are habitually greatly exaggerated. The diabolical lie is persistently affirmed, by enemies and morbid fanatics, that Christians are no better than others. A gross immorality which some professed Christian commits is trumpeted as proof, when the fact that it is seized upon and bruited is proof of the very opposite—that it is the exception; which proves that the rule is the other way.

The fact is that among the millions called Christians there are some hypocrites, and that some who were real Christians fall away into gross sins, and that it is so is what is to be expected. The hypocrite never did belong to the family. His proper place was outside, not inside, the fold. His hypocrisy simply shows that he was not properly classified, not proof that

Christians are hypocrites. The apostate ceases to be a Christian. The Church on the discovery of the fact spews them both out as soon as the facts are discovered.

What is true of evangelical churches of all denominations is that their communicants, while far from perfect, and while many of them give but little proof of regenerate life, are in heart and life characteristically, morally, and spiritually as differentiable from the unregenerate mass of men as day is from night. What Christian Church tolerates rogues, and harlots, and drunkards, and rum-sellers, and profane persons, and dissolute persons, or those guilty of any known immoralities? No; it is a defamation that the *visible* Church of God, even, is not distinguishable from the unbelieving world. Her altars are comparatively pure and her homes unsoiled. I have been intimately acquainted with the Church of all names, and carefully observant of her members in all parts of the world, for fifty years, and among the hundreds of thousands of whom I have had fair knowledge not a thousand have been detected in immoral practices, and such have been expelled upon detection. That discipline is often too low is not disputed; but that even is not so of immoralities but of minor practices, and faults about which there is difference of judgment as to how they should be dealt with lest too great rigor might destroy the wheat with the tares. The aim of the Church in the matter of a ruling purpose is that its members should be blameless, should abstain from all known sin, and love and revere God constantly and perfectly. In these fundamental aspects it is a comparatively holy Church. Its ministers are pure men; its influence is for righteousness; its services are divine; it stands as the breakwater against the incoming floods of sin; it stands for God and with God; it is the only organized power on earth that seeks to suppress all wrong and to recover men from the corruptions which destroy them. All this it does firmly, persistently, and with singleness of aim, at expense of labor and sacrifice. What of redeeming agency there is for the world, what there is for the betterment of mankind, flows from beneath her altars. To decry her and exaggerate her faults is to begrime and cripple the only organized agency on earth which supports the sinking hopes of mankind. So much must be kept in mind while we deal faithfully with the defects of Christians.

Christians are not perfect. This is a general fact of all Christians. Let us bravely look at the facts as they are painfully known to ourselves and as they appear in the light of a perfect standard. Christians are men. They are quarried from the common rock. In estimating them it must be remembered what they were—their blood and stock, and enviroments. There is marked diversity among Christians at the dawn of the divine consciousness and all the way along their after career. Some enter upon the Christian life with a clear and exultant experience, some with the simple consciousness of a desire and purpose to be Christians. This notes a great difference at the start. Some have an intelligent understanding of what their new life requires. Some have but a confused idea, with a strong impulse. There is difference of temperament, difference of intelligence, difference of personal habits in all respects. These facts inevitably carry over and result in different types of character and expression throughout life. Nature determines these diversities. In the spiritual, as in the natural, world there are occasional *lusus naturæ*—monstrosities.

Circumstances are influential, also—peculiarities of the people with whom the new-born soul finds itself associated; peculiarities of the sect notions and habits where its lot is cast; peculiarities of the pabulum on which it is fed; peculiarities of the ministry under which it is trained, the ideals which are set before it, and other things. There are general types which take on the denominational impress. It is not difficult to detect a Presbyterian, an Episcopalian, a Congregationalist, a Baptist, a Methodist, on slight acquaintance. But under all these types and diversities there is a family likeness, and the general and cardinal facts of experience are identical.

I note, first, among these common and cardinal facts of experience, beginning with regeneration and holding permanently throughout, a fixed desire and determination on the part of professed Christians to be true Christians—fixed, yet variable—stronger at one time than another. There are ebbs and flows in the spiritual tides. Sometimes faith becomes feeble and love grows cold, but they are not therefore extinguished. Doubtless many find their way into the churches without any profound spiritual experience, for one cause or another. They cannot be said to be Christians except in matters of external conformity with more or less strictness. Many such have been taught that this is all that is necessary. They aspire to nothing more. This is a grievous fault, but possibly even such derive some good and may even be led along to salvation. But among us, however it may be with sister Churches, there are but few who pass within the fold without a definite understanding that subjective experience is required, and a more or less distinct profession of having passed through such an experience. They are required to avow faith in Christ and a determination to lead a godly life. With rare exceptions they abstain from sinful practices and give proof of a prevailingly strong desire to be true disciples of Christ, but with variability. We regret to admit that the modern practice of many popular evangelists, of voting men to be Christians by a show of hands, has greatly damaged the average character of so-called Christians. Men are even asked to vote themselves in holiness. The standard of Christian experience has been sadly lowered by this superficial method.

There is continuity in Christian experience, and this is matter of experience. The defects which confessedly exist, while flaws and faults, do not wholly break up and abrogate the regenerate life. The will does not go over to unrighteousness. The relation between the soul and God is not dissevered. The branch is not plucked out of the vine, and never can be until it tears itself out by absolute sin and the volitional determination of itself to evil. With its inexcusable defects God is patient and long-suffering.

Some souls from the moment of their regeneration suffer no abatement. Their fervor never wanes, their love never grows cold. They go from strength to strength. It is not the rule, it must be confessed; but, while there are exceptions, it is the rule that the divine life, once implanted, abides. With faltering step, it may be, having entered upon the Christian course the soul pursues it to the end, or, falling away in some untoward hour and getting out of the fold, is almost certain to return.

I note, second, as a common fact of Christian experience, that the ideal varies with the ebbs and tides of the soul. Sometimes it is high, sometimes low; and there are corresponding differences in the external manifestation. Now there is joyousness, warmth, zeal, earnestness, intensity, high endeavor, strictness; anon there is lukewarmness, lethargy, laxity approaching indifference, self-indulgence, worldliness. Now the soul is borne along on a crest of triumph; now it is down in a trough of despondency, weak, irresolute, unhappy, discontented. Now the path is rocky and hard and the wilderness barren, and the flesh-pots are tempting and inviting; again, there is music and dancing and gladness in all the chambers of the soul; it is a feast-day in Zion, and all the windows are illuminated and banners flutter along the walls and turrets. When the ideal is high and the soul in its divinest mood the graces shine and duty and sacrifices and trials are easy; when it is otherwise duty is irksome and trials and sacrifices an intolerable burden.

I note, third, that dissatisfiedness of the soul with itself is a common experience of all regenerate souls, varying from intense distress at times to mild regret. Its experiences are not satisfactory. It has a prevailing consciousness of inexcusable defects. It does not reach its ideal. It feels the chidings of the Holy Spirit. It lashes itself with reprovings. It often carries an unhealed wound because of its unfaithfulness, or failure to be what it feels it ought to be. There is the abiding consciousness that there is something better for it. When it is upheld and sustained in an average experience, and others think well of it, and there is no external failure visible to other eyes, it discerns inward poverties which grieve and distress it. It would love more, be more patient, more brave, more trusting, more cheerful, stronger, more robust; it would work more and do more and be more. There are holy yearnings in it after something higher and nobler. There is often a distressing sense of remaining evil in it. I think I am safe in saying this is universal experience subsequent to the experience of regeneration.

This has been called in our theologizing and in the theologizing of all the Christian schools the "remains of the carnal mind," "unextracted roots of inbred sin," "the spirit of the flesh," "natural corruption," "seeds of depravity," "the old man," and by various other semi-scriptural names. These phrases all point to a fact, but not unfrequently a sensuous meaning is attached to them which leads wide apart from the truth which they aim to represent. They are supposed to represent some sediment or infusion in the soul or in the body, or in both, which must be washed out. What is meant and what is true is this: When the soul is forgiven, and its affections are turned to righteousness and its will is determined to the practice of righteousness, so that it passes from under the *dominion* of evil, impulses and inclination to evil are not completely eradicated. They still arise and assert themselves. They assail and disturb the peace of the soul. They have a constant tendency to prevail with it. They find support in its old habits and in its native lusts—that is, desires and cravings.

I note, fourth, that it accords with Christian experience that faithfulness keeps perennial sunshine in the soul. Watchfulness against the approaches of evil, a habit of the soul of constantly looking to God, not simply at critical moments, moments of trial and temptation, but at all times; scrupulous and conscientious attendance upon the services of the sanctuary, resistance of all suggestions of wrong, pronounced allegiance to Christ, smooth the path and make it easy and delightful, while all attempts at compromise with questionable practices make the way rough and thorny. The Christian soon learns that he cannot travel alone. He must have Christ with him. To have Christ with him he must keep in the path. The way is strait and narrow—the King's highway of holiness through a world of sin. There are lures and snares; he must avoid them. If he will he may be great and strong; if he will he may be weak and vacillating.

While there is a fundamental agreement in the phenomena of all soul regeneracy there is great and marked dissimilarity among Christians. One soul experiences and exhibits marked pre-eminence of some one or several graces, but no less marked defects as to other graces. Another soul reverses the order. Still another presents high or moderate attainments along the whole line of the graces. The mean average will perhaps not vary much except in extreme cases of either general defectiveness or general excellencies. May I, for the purpose of furnishing a mirror into which each reader may look and find something like himself, present several illustrations: A is a man of great faith; he is mighty in public prayer; his soul is easily roused to enthusiasm; but he is variable in temper, and, like a chameleon, takes the hue of his surroundings. He does not appear to advantage at the hustings or in the market. His indiscretions often trouble him. His best friends have to bear with him and apologize for him. B is a paragon of discretion—never offends good taste or good morals; is careful in the use of his tongue, and coldly proper as an icicle; but he is rarely present at the prayer-meeting, and his faith never kindles into enthusiasm. C is as honest as the heathen Cato; scrupulous to a line in business—his word is as good as his bond; but he is hard and unsympathetic in his family; his wife has no spending money, and his children dread his frown. D flourishes in an experience-meeting and is loud for spirituality, punctual to all the services, and zealous for revivals; but he is stingy and mean in charities, and leaves others to defray the expenses. E professes holiness, and wants a holiness-meeting once a week; but cares little for any thing else and wears out his minister and sets the neighborhood in strife by his uncharitable speeches and his selfish and unchristlike spirit. F is a bigot: a Methodist bigot, who glories in free grace and a universal atonement; a Baptist bigot, who thinks nobody unimmersed ought to be allowed the communion or can be saved; a Presbyterian bigot, who thinks the way to heaven leads through the Westminster

Confession, and is not certain that infants can be saved, and is quite certain that no heathen can; a Congregational bigot, that sees no possibility of grace outside the standing order; an Episcopal bigot, that considers it a damnable heresy not to believe in apostolical succession, but is uncharitable or worldly or self-indulgent.

These are the flies that spoil the ointment; the spiritual monstrosities that deform the bride of Christ and bring discredit on *his* fair name. No age has been without them, and no saintliest sect. Many of the individuals in these several genera without doubt are, in the root of the matter, Christians; they mean righteousness and loyalty; they have an experience of grace; in their deepest heart they love God, and they would not consort with sinners. They are simply malformations—like men with defective members. Meantime E, the general type, is a humble follower of Christ, who is gentle in his manners; kind and sympathetic in his spirit; true in all his business relations; faithful to his Church; careful and consistent in his walk; generous in his devisings for the poor; diligent in business, with an open hand for the support of every movement for the uplift of man ; but he makes little noise, and rarely speaks of himself. And F is a glorious Christian who loves God with all his heart, and dares to say it at suitable times, not boastingly, but confidently and humbly; and men believe it because of his sublime and godlike life. He loves the house of God, and his seat is never vacant without cause. He bears his share of the burdens cheerfully; if needs be, more. He is earnest for the salvation of the world; prays for it, and pays for it; holds up the hands of his minister with encouraging words and helpful deeds ; has sunshine in his face and in his soul—at home, in his place of business, and in the house of God; bears trials with equanimity; is unselfish, generous, and has a hand and heart full of charity. No envy or jealousy or ill feeling has a corner in his soul. He is never a self-inflated troubler of the church to which he belongs.

The course of Christian experience ought to be like "the path of the just, which shineth more and more unto the perfect day." There is every reason why it should be so—every thing to inspire it. The cause he has espoused and the experience he has had deserve and demand magnificent manhood. It ought to be impossible that he should be less than sublime. Why is it that this result does not follow? Simply the remaining power of old ideas and the corruption of the affections and enslavement of the will by them. There is still a contest carried on in the soul as to who shall reign. It tolerates the controversy. It says God shall reign. It will not entertain the idea of the dominion of its old and now dethroned master; but it has not faith or courage enough to determine on their absolute expulsion. It is confused as to how much indulgence may be allowed them. They make constant encroachments. There is schism where there ought to be harmony. Conscience illuminated by the Holy Spirit says one thing; desire of the flesh and the world say another. The will plays fast and loose between the opposing forces. It will not go over to unrighteousness, but it will not decide for ideal righteousness. It will not sin, but it will dally. It is determined not to yield to temptation, but it often makes a weak resistance. It has burned the bridges, but at times it half inclines to rebuild them. It has not strength to push away from the borders of the enemy's country; but sometimes lingers with a half-craving look to the apples of Sodom and the fleshpots of Egypt. There is a pull both ways in it—with an occasional inclination to compromise. It despises gross sin, but it courts some indulgence. God wants the soul; he gives the larger half.

From all this it will appear that average Christian experience is not unalloyed. It is not the experience of an ideally perfect soul. There are none such on earth, and never will be. That estate belongs to the world to which Christian experience leads. It is the experience of an exile far from home with an intervening wilderness to pass; of a soul beleaguered by foes; of a soul in the furnace of trial; of a soul on the field of battle. It is not a perfectly happy experience. The actual experience has its griefs and sorrows and heart-aches—its defeats with its victories. But its *griefs* are better than the joys of sin; it is better to suffer affliction with the people of God, if need be, than to enjoy the pleasures of sin for a season. It is better to lie wounded, and even to die, wrapped in a flag of loyalty than to ride in a chariot with the brand of treason. There is happiness in the pursuit and aspirations after righteousness, despite all the trials, which must forever be unknown to souls under the bondage of sin. This happiness comes to every sincere soul, in the conscious peace and safety of a life of faith—"the peace of God that passeth understanding."

But is there not something better for the Christian soul than the defective experience I have described? I unhesitatingly answer, Yes. The possibilities of grace are not exhausted in an average experience. The common defects are not necessary, and they are not excusable. They are defects—flaws and faults which may be and ought to be remedied. The soul is convalescent, with promises of perfect healing if it will, but the cure is not complete. The goal of perfect health has not been reached. It is a forgiven soul, and so delivered from guilt. It is a regenerate soul, having in it initial restoratives to normalcy—the actual presence of the divine life in it—but it has remaining defects, flaws and faults, which demand further cure, and for the want of which it does not enjoy continuous sunshine, but often suffers chidings of conscience and reproof of the blessed Holy Spirit.

Now, I think, any candid and intelligent Christian will admit that these facts are the general facts of Christian experience. What' is the philosophy of these facts; that is, what is the rational explanation of them? To this question I must answer, first, it is not because a better experience is not possible. I think I am safe in saying that there is no Christian soul, whatever its attainments in grace, that does not feel that it has not exhausted the possibilities of grace. I think we must all agree that any remaining defect is not on God's part. His part of the work is not imperfect. The forgiveness is a perfect forgiveness. The seed of the divine life implanted is a perfect seed. He has furnished all the conditions requisite on his part for a perfect result—so far as a perfect result can be reached. His spirit has come into the soul to restore it, and realize in it complete harmony with its law, if it will.

My second affirmation is, that any remaining defectiveness of experience is the fault of the soul itself. That fault is either a curable fault or it is not. If it is not curable, it must arise from the nature of the subject; that is, must be because the subject will not admit of any thing more perfect. That is a conceivable fact. There is a limit to the possibilities of the finite. But if this be the case, the defect cannot involve blameworthiness in any sense. For not to realize the impossible can violate no ethical obligation. But if it is a curable defect, it must be curable either by the soul itself, or by God, who is the co-factor, or by both conjointly. If it is curable by the soul itself, then the soul is at fault. If it is curable by God himself, and if it ought to be cured, then God is at fault. This is an impossible thought. But if it is curable by God and the soul conjointly, then the fault must fall upon both or upon one of the co-factors. It is impossible to think that God is at fault. Then the fault must still be with the soul for some failure on its part, which acts as a hinderance to God in doing what he would do for it if it were faithful to prescribed conditions. If God does not do all that he might do if the soul contributed its conditioning part the responsibility still falls on the soul. Its experience is defective because it will have it so, or because in some way, from an infirmity which it fails to overcome or which cannot be overcome, it does not furnish the conditions of a more perfect experience.

LECTURE VIII.

POSSIBILITIES OF GRACE, AND ADVICES.

Can ordinary Christian experience be improved? We unhesitatingly answer, yes. Ought it to be improved? Again we unhesitatingly, answer, yes. When may it be improved? We unhesitatingly answer, now; and continuously evermore. In what respects and how may it be improved? This will require more extended answer.

I approach the question, In what respect and how may the experience of a regenerate soul be improved by the postulation of a law?

All movements in the spiritual world, as in the natural, are regulated by law—nothing is left to accident or the hazard of chance. God is a God of order. He regulates his own movements according to perfect rules, which he never violates. They are as fixed and immutable as his own nature and infinite perfections.

Natural science is unraveling the mysteries of nature simply by ascertaining the fixed and unalterable laws. Spiritualistic science must pursue the same method. The problem is more involved, but, we must believe, not absolutely insoluble. The regulating law may be found by a profound study of the soul, with the aid of the reflected light of revelation.

We begin with the statement that a spirit is a real being and a perfectly definite being—as absolutely so as any other being. Nothing in nature is in any respect more real. As a being, a spirit is exactly what God made it—nothing more—nothing less—nothing other. As a being it has added nothing to itself and can add nothing. In this respect it is as powerless as any material atom. There may be varied types of spiritual beings, each differing from all others in degrees and kinds of powers, for aught we know; but each type, and each individual under the type, has, as to content of being, precisely the dower imparted in creation. As to the powers and attributes with which it is endowed, therefore, and as to the environments in which it finds itself placed, it can have no more responsibility than any other atom has. This is our first postulate.

The human soul, whose experiences are the subject of our inquiry, is better known to us than any other spirit, and in some respects better known to us than any other being. No knowledge is so certain as that which is given in consciousness. The soul—its powers, states, acts, and laws of action—is the immediate subject of consciousness. By consciousness we know the existence of soul—the direct cognition of it emerges in every other knowledge. We know it as the *ego*—the self and every other object, including the body, as objective—as the not-self—as external. In the same way, by consciousness, we know that the self is unknown to consciousness, as possessing any of the qualities we perceive in material objects, as form, color, weight, divisibility, and such like. We know that, while void of these qualities, the self knows itself as possessing other qualities which material objects do not possess, or are not perceived to possess. These qualities are, power to know, including the intellectual group—to perceive, to form ideas, to think, to reason, to differentiate, to compare, to judge, to remember, to distinguish between what things are true and what are fanciful; power of imagination and faith; powers of sensibility—the sensitive and emotive group—as power to love and hate, to feel joy and sorrow, approbation and remorse, pain and pleasure; the moral group—power to distinguish between right and wrong, to feel the obligation of the ought and ought not, to feel the counter attractions of objects known to be right or wrong; the voluntary group—power to choose between objects which are discerned to be right or wrong, power of free self-determination to this or that or the other ; to make good or evil choices, to obey or disobey the imperative of righteous laws.

If there is any thing known, so much the ego knows of itself. The soul is able to know still more than these qualities, attributes, powers, or whatsoever you choose to call them, of itself. It cognizes certain laws of relation and interaction among these several groups of powers, regulative of them—an inner and inviolable constitution or economy of its life. While it knows that all these groups of powers have a unitary ground, that is, that the self is one and indivisible, it knows that the groups of powers act separately, but under law, and each group under its own law, and that the interaction of the several groups among and upon each other is under a predetermined law also, which never is and never can be violated by itself, and which its creator will never disregard. Under this sacred constitution the intellectual group of powers takes the initiative in every movement. The movement may stop here, and neither the natural or moral sensibilities participate at all—may not at all be called into exercise. The mind perceives, judges, fancies, remembers—that is all. No sensibility is excited, no emotion stirred. An object has passed before it, but has aroused no passion, no desire, no feeling. When the sensibilities are untouched the voluntary group cannot be brought into exercise. In order to this, some emotive condition must supervene. The second group must in some way be touched before the third can be brought into exercise.

In order to bring the second group into exercise, it is requisite not only that there should be an exercise of the first, but the object which passes before the first group must have power to interest the second in some way and to some degree—must start some emotion of desire, fear, curiosity, or interest of some kind—otherwise, it will pass simply as a shadow over the landscape.

Now, it is under the operation of this law that God develops ethical states in the soul of man; it is by means of it that he expels evil and enthrones holiness. Careful examination will discern in this law the solution of the problem of regeneration and of soul progress toward perfection. To expel the false he introduces the true; to win from the evil he presents the good. He sets life and death before the soul, that it may choose which. He quickens and energizes by means of the truth. It is what has been aptly called "the expulsive power of a new affection." In regeneration he creates a preponderance of affection toward righteousness. He draws the soul by a new attraction. The will becomes empowered to reverse its former choices and determine upon a new course. The spiritual currents set in a new direction. A new life dominates. The soul is revolutionized—born anew. The whole tenor of practice is changed.

We have said the defects of experience after regeneration are of two kinds: First, in the matter of the subjective state of the soul; second, in the matter of external manifestation.

The status of the soul after regeneration has been already described at length, and it is only necessary to make a brief *résumé* here. It is a forgiven soul with the principle of righteousness implanted in it, but it has the evil of infirmity, of weakness, and strong tendencies to sin remaining in it, as the heirloom of its native abnormalcy or depravity; and, further than that, tendencies to sin which have grown in it by indulgence and by the free choice of evil which has marked its previous life. The throb of the divine life in it is feeble and subject to fluctuations. There is not only weakness but also poverty in its graces. Infancy implies all this. All Christians are conscious of it. Some infants are more robust than others; some are sickly and do not grow. Growth is not determined by time merely, but also by health and nutritious food. The soul, like the body, needs good constitution, rich blood, to begin with; wants to be well born; it also wants care and nutrition. Truth makes some tissue. Aspiration opens all the avenues to light and warmth. Prayer brings needed supplies. Where these are wanting life pulses feebly and emaciation is painfully visible. There are many sickly souls—not entirely dead, but only just alive. This is not a desirable state. Who is content with weakness and poverty of blood? Who does not see beauty in the ruddy glow and the strong elastic movement?

The other defect we mentioned is that of the life. This follows the other. If the inward life is feeble the outward will be sure to be careless, irregular, unsatisfactory. The stream will not rise above the fountain. There is interaction between the internal and external. A cold heart, absence of inner strength, will manifest itself in the practical life and outward example. So also unfaithfulness in the outward life will bring death to the soul. Fidelity in externals will help to the creation and preservation of internal health, and the contrary.

We now raise the question, Can these defects be removed, or in any degree removed; and, if so, *how* and *when?*

This is a subject among us of great importance as affecting the peace of the Church and as affecting the question what we are to teach as truth.

Can the defect be removed, or in any degree be removed? No one pretends that any amount of gracious agency that may be exerted in the soul can lift it into a state of absolute perfection, or angelic perfection, or even Adamic perfection, though there is a total absence of proof that Adamic perfection rated very high. Thus by common consent a damage has come to the soul by sin that in some respects is irreparable while it remains in the body. All admit that as a soul, in the matter of the right adjustment of its affections and development of its intelligence and strength and proper action of its will, it is capable of great and progressive improvement. Some believe, and even assert it as matter of personal experience, that following regeneration, by a special and separate act of the Holy Ghost, in answer to prayer and a faith which claims it, the soul may immediately and consciously be raised to a state in which all evil tendencies will be eradicated and all temptations cease to have any influence with it. Others believe that by continuous growth it may ultimately come into this state while yet in the body. But even those who hold this high view do not pretend that, while rendered ethically perfect, it is freed from infirmities of judgment or delivered from defects which do no affect character.

All along through the Christian ages there have been Johannine spirits of such saintliness as to give sanction to the most extreme views as to the possibilities of grace. Thomas à Kempis, Fénelon, Fletcher, Madame Guyon, and others dead, and some still living might be added to the list. For more than a hundred years it has been a subject of deep interest among Christians of mystical tendencies in all sects, and especially among the Methodist family of churches. It has undoubtedly given rise to fanaticisms and delusions in an alarming degree.

Meantime there is a great truth which must be conserved, and, as far as possible, rescued from the abuses to which it has become subjected. The odium that gathers about it by evil association is no excuse for its desertion. Christ, if on the gibbet, is still Christ. A jewel is still a jewel however incrusted with base alloys. The alloys may hide the precious gem or disfigure its beauty, but cannot destroy its value. It is the task of Christian patience to remove the debasing incrustations and set it in position.

The truth to be preserved is that there is a higher experience possible to Christians than that which is attained in and at the time of regeneration; and this must be so taught as not to reflect discredit on regeneration on the one hand or excite fanaticism on the other, and so as to inspire aspiration after it as duty and privilege. The possibility of enlargement is beyond question. The duty is plain. The desire is felt by every truly regenerate soul. It may and ought to be by growth in grace day by day. It may be by sudden and overwhelming manifestations to and in the soul at any moment when earnestly sought. It is precisely the same grace of life in all stages of possible enlargement—God more and more, or in a moment, completely filling the regenerate soul with his presence and his love, so that it effloresces in all the graces of righteousness; its love is perfect and its peace is undisturbed.

There is such an enlargement possible, and we must believe it is possible at any moment. There is no limit to the possibilities of grace short of the perfect love which keeps perpetual sunshine of God's favor. The limits are in ourselves. God wills that his people should be a holy people; that every facet of the saved soul should reflect his image; that the seed of life implanted in it should grow to a tree of righteousness, every bough of which should come to perfect fruitage. He would have all his soldiers valiant, all his saints appearing before the Lord and going from strength to strength. He would have no schisms in the ranks and no laggards in the march. He would see all clothed in the beautiful garments of meekness, gentleness, and love. He would have a glorious Church, without spot or wrinkle, whose priests are clothed with salvation and whose saints shout aloud for joy. He would have his Zion a city set on a hill whose glory cannot be hid, and whose shining would lighten the nations. For this he would have each soul filled with the glory and joy of his presence —a sacred temple all of whose recesses are undefiled. We are sure that this is so. There is no Christian soul that does not feel that it is so. It is the ringing cry resounding through all the corridors of every Christian soul: "Be ye holy that bear the vessels of the Lord."

What is this higher grace? Some call it holiness; some purity; some sanctification; some perfection; some maturity. There has been much unseemly disputation over the name as well as much fanatical profession concerning the experience, and much crude and unsound teaching as to what it includes and how it is to be attained, and much ill-tempered criticism.

It answers all the ends of description to say it is the perfecting of the soul in love. Love is not simply the queen of the graces, but the mother of them all—the all-embracing. Love is the fulfilling of the law; love made perfect excludes envy, jealousy, pride, and all violent and hurtful tempers and acts; love is reverent, meek, humble, docile, patient, obedient, worketh no ill, fulfilleth all righteousness. Perfect love inspires perfect faith, courage, heroism, self-denial, casteth out all fear. Perfection of holy love is the perfection of saintship. The cultivation of every other grace is prompted by love, and all growth in them is measured by and is heightening of love. Love to God is a divine inspiration. God fills the soul with his love to overflowing. It thrills with gladness. It expels impurity. While it reigns there is no place for evil thoughts, evil desires, evil feelings. Heaven has already come. Can it be permanent at its highest pitch? We think we are safe in saying not, as an emotion. The thrill of love and joy must be intermittent in a life like ours on the earth. Other feelings must come and for the time obscure and replace these. But as a principle governing the life we are bold to say love may and should abide moment by moment and without alloy. That is all God wants; that is moral perfection; that is spiritual holiness; that opens heaven. Heaven will differ from the present as simple fullness of all that love implies, with nothing to interrupt its expression and nothing to detract from its rapture—no jar, no abatement, no alloy—love inspiring, directing, thrilling every power for ever and ever.

How may this better experience be attained? To this we answer, just as all spiritual experience is attained: by the proper action of the soul itself and the co-working of God with it. It will not be forced; it will not come unsought; it will not come improperly sought. Mere desires or mere prayers or mere faith will not secure it. External reforms or mere legal morality will not bring it. There are no artificial means or magical appliances that will help to it. Professions do not aid to it. It is not an esoteric trust conferred by some sanctified guild; it is not necessary outcome of lapse of time; it is not a reserved grace to be realized only in the dying hour.

God's methods with the soul are normal. Soul development is according to fixed and unalterable laws. That the soul come into its highest possibilities, what is necessary on the soul's part?

First, it is necessary that it should have before it a distinct aim and a definite ideal. The general aim must be the attainment of the highest excellence of Christian character, as near an approach as possible to ideal perfection. The initial aim of the seeking soul was forgiveness, deliverance from guilt. This is the starting-point of all Christian experience. Hence the struggle of repentance and faith. In forgiveness and regeneration it attains this primary aim, comes to the beginning of a holy character. But now another goal opens to it—the goal of perfected holiness, a life according to the divine ideal. Every renewed soul comes to feel not only that it has not fully attained, but an impulse of desire and a sense of obligation to the continued pursuit of something more. What that something more is should be resolutely studied. The soul must be induced to see and feel its defects and to consider the possibilities of grace and the obligation to reach them to the utmost. It is not a difficult thing to find what the defects are. As a rule they are open. The soul sees and feels them—its weaknesses, its failures, its shortcomings, its want of utter devotion —remaining earthliness, leasing after questionable pleasures— moral defects and blemishes, not willful sins, but not a satisfying freedom from evil impulses—a low average grade of spiritual life. It must by attention to the chidings of the Spirit, to the calls of conscience, to the holy yearnings within in its best moments keep ever seeking. It must be earnest to keep the highest ideal before it, however it may feel rebuked by it. This is God's appointed method of soul growth. He puts the standard before the soul and demands that it shall measure itself by it and measure its obligations by it. It must be loyal to the test. This is the finger-boarded road. The end to be aimed at we must remember is not a feeling, but a life; not a shibboleth, but a character—a perfect cleansing of the heart from all sinful indulgence.

The second point is a resolute determination to measure up to the divine standard—the ideal. It will cost something, but it is enough that God demands it, and both consistency and the soul's peace, and the greatest usefulness demand it. No headway can be made without fixed purpose. The soul must say, I will by God's help. The resolution must be final—absolute. There must be no compromise. God covets the whole heart.

Third. These conditions being met, the prayer of faith will win the evermore increasing consciousness of completeness in Christ; love will be enthroned; more and more peace and every other grace will abound; the soul will be filled with the fullness of God's love and will reflect his image. God's time is now, and every succeeding now. There is no need that we dispute about names. What the demand is and must ever be from day to day is holiness to the Lord—all of grace that absolute consecration of our whole being and present faith will bring us. Soul hunger and simple faith are our part. It is God's part to cleanse the temple and fill it with his glory.

To keep any grace bestowed the soul must be alert. "Keep the soul with all diligence, for out of it are the issues of life," is God's exhortation. As you see, synergism runs through from beginning to end of the whole process. God keeps only those who keep themselves. "Watch and pray, lest ye enter into temptation," is the command. "The Lord is thy keeper" is the encouragement. Nothing is so delicate as the purity of the soul—a breath of evil soils it. Contagion and pollution are in the earthly air; temptation lurks in every ambush. Every motive needs to be scanned, every thought scrutinized, every feeling noted, the will vigilant and prompt to every duty. The heart must be kept clear from envy, evil imaginations and surmisings—selfishness, pride, self-will—must cultivate meekness, docility, charity, humility, reverence, prayerfulness, faith—in honor preferring others; must see that love has absolute empire. The tongue, that unruly member, must be kept under constant espionage. The life must be pure, brave, generous, self-denying, full of good deeds and beautiful sanctities, void of strifes and contentions. The way is narrow and strait, "the king's highway of holiness"; but with the constant supplies of God help, which faith and prayer will bring, it can be traveled, and perpetual sunshine will gladden the pilgrim soul who keeps it. Growth is God's order. No stage is or can ever be reached when the divine order is excluded or superseded. The more vigorous the life implanted the more constant and marked should be the growth. Each new advance is the stage for another. "From the blade to the full corn in the ear"—from childhood to manhood, and ever more and more perfect manhood. Faith, prayer, watchfulness, diligence, absolute purpose, are the divine conditions of success—holiness the goal.

There is no such thing as growth or even continuance in grace without the continuous use of the acquired power. The law of increase, or even continued possession, is use. The parable of the talents. It is the universal law: "He that hath [that is, he that uses] to him shall be given"—use makes increase. "Not the hearer but the doer of the law" is the approved servant. An unused talent shrivels and dies. It is important that we should not make mistake what is use. It is not use simply to be punctual to church, or even to private prayer and heart searching, or loud and constant testimony and profession. The public services of the Church are means of grace, and so of prayer and heart searching. Rightly used they give tone and strength, but they are the arsenal, the armory. They exist as means to an end. Holy living is the end. If we would grow in this we must use the strength derived, not merely enjoy it. It is the use that gives zest. Grace is given that we may act, not simply be happy. Holiness to the Lord means co-working with God. "If any man love me he will keep my commandments." He that is patient, industrious, generous, charitable, busy doing good, earnest in right living, will be the thrifty growing plant in the garden of the Lord.

I quote from Dr. Roswell Dwight Hitchcock's *Eternal Atonement*, a little volume of great beauty and in which is a large amount of useful reading : " What then is God's will? So far as we ourselves are concerned this is the will of God, says an apostle, even our sanctification. That we advance in holiness, subduing our sins, that we grow every day more pure, more fruitful, more like Christ, our pattern—this is the will of God concerning us. It is the making our religion not an entertainment, but a service. We are to set before us the perfect standard and then struggle to shape our lives to it. Personal sanctity must be made a business of. Those saints of the Middle Ages, like Tauler and à Kempis, who wrestled so hard for holiness, slaying so sternly their bosom sins and looking so meekly yet so fixedly to Christ, may well be invoked as the rebukers of our sloth. It is just at this point that the piety of our day is the most sadly defective. It is not sufficiently inflamed with a desire after sanctity. It is self-indulgent when it ought to be self-denying—tolerant of impurities and infirmities of which it ought to be utterly intolerant; cold and slack, when it ought to be warm and diligent; asleep over faults of character and in the presence of spiritual dangers which ought to awaken godly jealousy and godly fear. It is true we are saved by hope, and yet it is equally true that he who hath this hope in him should purify himself, as Christ is pure. In a word, it is character that is required of us; laid, indeed, in grace and imperfect at the best, needing to shelter itself behind the perfect righteousness of Christ, yet a piece of solid moral masonry to be carried on and carried up by a life-long toil; and this, too, not for our own sake, but for Christ's sake and because God so wills it. Our own spiritual comfort, the sure fruit of a careful walk with God, though an incident, is not to be the end of our endeavors, but all we do is to be out of simple loyalty to redeeming love. Mere obedience to conscience is but a pagan virtue, which in the highest sphere is not a virtue at all. Virtue for us is obedience to God in Christ. Painstaking, of course, it will be, that there may be no blot upon the life; self-denying, as against our indulgence, our appetites, and our passions; asking only for duty, though we knew it were asking for martyrdom; and all for Christ. Such is the will of God concerning us, and only he who does it should reckon himself a child of God.

"But besides this resolute endeavor after personal sanctity we have duties also toward our Christian brethren. The fellowship of the saints, the Church catholic on earth, under whatever name or forms, as widely reaching as Christendom itself—these are the only permitted boundaries of our love. Wheresoever Christ has gone with his quickening grace there must we also follow with the mantle of Christian charity. They who love a common Lord must love each other." *

We have now sufficiently indicated the facts and processes of Christian experience in their order and relation and the underlying implications. So far forth we have reached a philosophy of them—that is, a rational explanation of them. We have seen that they accord with fundamental moral and mental laws. It remains that we more particularly point out the reason why of them—the end they serve. This has been implied all along, but perhaps should be more carefully stated.

It is a safe principle to assume that nothing in the divine

*Eternal Atonement, pp. 47, 48.

economy is without an adequate end. Wherefore all this arrangement?

To this we answer in general terms, it is God's plan of bringing men to eternal holy happiness. Man is a sinner; this is God's way of saving him—that is, of rescuing him from the evils of sin. We make two points: First, there is no other way; second, this is a rational and effectual way. Let any one seriously raise the question how man can be saved from sin, and he will soon discover that he has a difficult problem on hand. He will find that sin involves character and not merely external conduct; that at its root it is rebellion against God; resistance of all ethical laws; hostility to the person and plans of the Almighty Sovereign of the universe; anarchy, ruin, death.

How shall it be got rid of? Character cannot be forced. It cannot be created by omnipotent will without annihilating the moral system. The principle of administration that would uproot sin by force would at the same time uproot holiness—the possibility of it. The omnipotent force that would coerce a will would in the act obliterate the moral system.

He cannot ignore sin, and treat it as he treats holiness. Let any one try to think it and he will be compelled to discover that it is impossible. God has no power to obliterate moral distinctions, so that sin and holiness shall be identical, or be treated as identical. Ethical principles are simply the immutable principles of his own eternal holiness. To change them or ignore them would be to overthrow himself.

There is no salvation by mere sovereignty.

The problem is to get rid of sin—to change the sinner to a saint; to make him such a being as a holy God can love. So to revolutionize him that holy law can approve him, and holy beings associate with him, and holy happiness come to him.

His impure thoughts must be taken out of him, his unholy nature must be changed, his rebellious will must be made loyal, his malice and selfishness must be replaced with love, he must be put into harmony with heaven's people and heaven's law, and heaven's spirit, and heaven's practices. There is no other way to save him.

Christian experience is God's way of solving the problem, his appointed method of reaching the end. We have seen what that method is. We have seen that it violates no ethical law; that it does not require the surrender of holiness on God's part and that it does no violence to the freedom of man, and that it imperils no interest of the universe—that it honors eternal justice and eternal love. It is a process which not only may issue in salvation—that is, not only furnishes a rational ground for salvation, but on ethical principles must issue in salvation. He that was a sinner, and as such was of ethical necessity excluded from heaven, which is but another name for holy happiness, by the change wrought in him becomes not only fitted for heaven, but on eternal ethical principles cannot be excluded from heaven. The change through which he has passed was exactly that which was needed—the means answer to the end, as any effect answers to its cause.

In bringing the lectures on the philosophy of Christian experience to a close a few advices may not be out of place.

There is not a Christian among us, whether in the pulpit or in the pew, that does not feel that what God wants is a holy Church; that the bride of his Son should be spotless; that Zion should shine; that a sinless age should come.

The pulpit is God's great instrument for the accomplishment of these results. What is needed in these times is that the pulpit should be faithful. More and more let it sound the note of warning to the sinful generation. This must continue to be its chief function. It is "the ministry of reconciliation." Its commission is to warn, to persuade sinful men to flee from the wrath to come, and to build up the Church of believers in holy faith. Let it be true to its commission. Let it sound the note of warning, "dividing the word of its message faithfully, giving to saint and sinner each his portion in due season"—"cry aloud and spare not."

The messenger of God should be wise. There never was a time when more wisdom was needed. There are many lo! heres and lo! theres. Go not after them. Follow the only safe guide—the great Teacher himself. Preach the word: the whole word; be instant in season and out of season. Avoid things that engender strife, contention, and unprofitable disputation. Cater to no party or prejudice. Keep the spirit of love and gentleness. Feed the flock; do not neglect the lambs. Preach not to please yourselves, but the Master whose servants you are. Beware lest your words and doctrines engender mischief. "Study to show yourselves approved of God, workmen that need not to be ashamed." Be not censorious in the pulpit. Keep ever in mind that when you season your words with bitterness the harvest will not be sweet. Do not imagine that you can minister to life with tempers and words that lacerate and wound those whom you are sent to heal. Let it not be that the people who shall sit under your ministry shall, under the inspiration of your temper and teachings, be torn by divisions and factions. Heal the wounds and bind up the sores of the hurt of God's people.

Preach the great doctrine of holiness, not technically or disputatiously, but in the spirit of love; not to repel, but to attract and win. Preach it naturally, as you preach every other truth. Let it live and breathe through all your teachings and in all

your services in due proportion and out of the heart of love.
Avoid unholy holiness. Encourage aspiration after a beautiful
and blameless life. Let your gospel so build men in truth and
love and all your services so be intoned with unction of sacredness that hungry souls will be fed, and that cravings after less
nutritious food will find no occasion. Deal gently with the weak
and erring. Aspire, yourselves, after greatest sacredness of
character—the highest soul experience. Set an example of
meekness and modesty in your own professions, and of true and
sublime character in your devotion to the work which has been
committed to you. Remember the maxim, "like priest, like
people," and be an example to the flock.

A word of advice to those believers who do not make great
professions of attainments in grace. You profess to be Christians. That itself is a great profession. It places you among the
children of God. It brings you under the obligations of a
righteous and holy life. Recognize that fact. Especially
beware of thinking it a praiseworthy thing—a virtue—not to
profess much. More yet, beware of imagining that it lessens your
obligation to a holy heart and a holy life; rather lament the
conscious deficiencies which restrain you. Above all, do not
allow yourselves to take an attitude of hostility to high experience because you do not yourself enjoy it, or because of prejudice against some who seem immodest, and whose lives, to your
thinking, contradict their professions. Justify not your delinquencies because of their unseemliness. Think of the noble
examples of the best saints. Be charitable and forbearing. Do
not permit the frailties of others to be a hinderance to you.
Deal faithfully with your own soul. Remember you are a disciple of Christ; you represent him before men; you bear his
name; no man can stand for you; no man's delinquencies can

excuse you. Do not scandalize him by your unfaithfulness. If it is modesty that restrains you, pity the forward; if it is conscious shortcomings, be not censorious of others, but be quick to remedy your own faults. Remember your obligations; do not forget your responsibility. See to it that your example is faultless. Be not content with any thing short of utmost salvation.

A word to those who profess extraordinary attainments.

To begin with, remember there is no difference between you and your brethren that marks an essential distinction. You are brethren in the Lord—servants of the same Master, participants of the same life, members of the same family, journeying to the same heaven. Why should you fall out by the way and vex one another? The difference is one of more or less experience, not one of kind.

Have you more grace; have you experienced more of the deep things of God; is your brother less advanced? Then the greater reason that you should be gentle and kind. You have been lifted into a great experience; to you has been revealed more of the deep things of God; a deeper life has come into your soul.

Is there not reason that this great experience should make you an example of every grace? and more especially of the grace of humility and self-forgettingness? If God has filled you thus with his wondrous love, ought it not make your love more abounding? If you have tasted this grace I know you feel so.

You will receive kindly some advices, I am sure, if you are persuaded they are well meant, and I am sure what is here said is well meant. God wants a holy Church. The want of the age is a holy Church. The provisions of grace are adequate for a holy Church. Every effort possible ought to be employed to bring the Church up to the highest standard.

You love holiness. The first advice I offer is, love it more and more; still continue to aspire after its greater depths and heights; you cannot be too holy; but do not make the mistake of imagining that the profession of holiness is holiness, or is a means to its attainment or a means to its continuance. Above all avoid extravagance in the manner and terms of profession. This has been and yet is a source of great evil. There is no occasion for it. Your heart compels you to confess what God has done for you. That is right, but you want to be wise in the manner of your confession, and your life to correspond with it; otherwise it becomes an offense and does immense harm. Great mischief has come to the Church from this source. If your experience is genuine you would not do harm—make not your godliness itself an offense. It will not hurt you to be modest in speaking of yourself, to remember that you are fallible—not to think more highly of yourself than you ought to think; in honor to prefer others. Remember that self distrust is not a vice but a virtue rather. Remember further that any experience you may have had has not freed you from common infirmities, and therefore the reason for modesty. It is a comely and winning grace. Your fellow Christians who know you will, if your life accords with it, rejoice to hear, and will profit by, any profession you make if it be not extravagant in manner and word. Your speech and your experience will be to edification when inspired by love—never without such seasoning. There are noticeable tendencies which admonish you. Will you give heed?

That there are tendencies to overprofession, separation, spiritual egotism, pride, antinomianism, a freeing from the common law of duty, schism of the body of Christ, uncharitable judging of others, setting up a censorship over the pulpit, self-assertion and overweening confidence, a depreciation of the ordinary means of grace, fanaticism, no one who is observant can doubt.

Every thoughtful Christian knows that these dangers are rife. You may not be conscious of them in yourself, but you know they exist. This ought to be sufficient to put you on your guard.

I append Mr. Wesley's letter to Mr. Maxfield. You will see its appropriateness to our times:

JOHN WESLEY ON SANCTIFICATION.

The following characteristic letter from Mr. Wesley to Mr. Maxfield is found in Moore's *Life of Wesley:*

"Without any preface or ceremony, which is useless between you and me, I will simply and plainly tell you what I dislike in your doctrine, spirit, or outward behavior.

"1. I like your doctrine of perfection, or pure love—love excluding sin; your insisting that it is merely by faith; that consequently it is instantaneous (though preceded and followed by a gradual work), and that it may be now, at this instant. But I dislike your saying that a man may be as perfect as an angel; that he can be absolutely perfect, that he can be infallible, or above being tempted; or that the moment he is pure in heart he cannot fall from it.

"I dislike your directly or indirectly depreciating justification, saying a justified person is not in Christ, is not born of God, is not sanctified, not a temple of the Holy Ghost, or that he cannot please God, or cannot grow in grace.

"I dislike your saying that one saved from sin needs nothing more than looking to Jesus, needs not to hear or think of any thing else; believe, believe, is enough; that he needs no self-examination, no times of private prayer; needs not mind little or outward things; and that he cannot be taught by any person who is not in the same state.

"I dislike your affirming that justified persons in general

persecute them that are saved from sin, and that they have persecuted you on this account.

"2. As to your spirit, I like your confidence in God and your zeal for the salvation of souls.

"I dislike something which has the appearance of pride, of overvaluing yourselves and undervaluing others, particularly the preachers, thinking that not only are they blind, and that they are not sent of God, but even that they are dead—dead to God, and walking in the way to hell; that they are going one one way, you another; that they have no life in them; your speaking of yourselves as though you were the only men who knew and taught the Gospel; and as if not only all clergy, but all the Methodists besides, were in utter darkness.

"I dislike something that has the appearance of enthusiasm; overvaluing feeling and inward impressions; mistaking the mere work of imagination for the voice of the Spirit; expecting the end without the means, and undervaluing reason, knowledge, and wisdom in general.

"I dislike something that has the appearance of antinomianism; not magnifying the law and making it honorable; not enough valuing tenderness of conscience and exact watchfulness in order thereto; using faith rather as contradistinguished from holiness than as productive of it.

"But what I most of all dislike is your littleness of love to your brethren; your want of meekness, gentleness, long-suffering; your impatience of contradiction, counting every man your enemy that reproves or admonishes you in love; your bigotry and narrowness of spirit, loving, in a manner, only those that love you; your censoriousness, proneness to think hardly of all who do not earnestly agree with you; in one word, your divisive spirit. Indeed, I do not believe that any of you either design or desire a separation. But you do not enough fear, abhor, and detest it, shuddering at the very thought. All the preceding tempers tend to it, and gradually prepare you for it.

"3. As to your outward behavior, I like the general tenor of your life, devoted to God and spent in doing good.

"I dislike your appointing such meetings as hinder others from attending either the public preaching, or their class, or band.

"I dislike your spending so much time in several meetings as many that attend can ill spare from the other duties of their calling, unless they omit either the preaching, or their class, or band. This naturally tends to dissolve our society by cutting the sinews of it.

"As to more public meetings, I like the praying fervently and largely for all the blessings of God. I know much good has been done hereby, and I hope much more will be done. But I dislike several things therein: The using improper expressions in prayer, sometimes too bold, if not irreverent; sometimes too pompous and magnificent, extolling yourselves rather than God, and telling him what you are, not what you want. Your affirming people will be justified or sanctified just now. Your affirming they are, when they are not. The bidding them say, 'I believe.' The bitterly condemning any that oppose, calling them wolves, etc., and pronouncing them hypocrites or not justified.

"Read this calmly and impartially before the Lord in prayer. So shall the evil cease and the good remain. And you will then be more than ever united to

"Your affectionate brother, J. WESLEY.
"CANTERBURY, *Nov.* 2, 1762."

I cannot close this discussion without adding to these wise and admonitory words of Mr. Wesley—words which were necessary in his time, and which show how sorely he was troubled with disturbers in his day by the unskillful handling of the great doctrine he taught, a further admonition demanded in our time from the same cause: I do so with unfeigned humility and, I am sure, in the spirit of sincere love—in the spirit of our common Master. There can be but one aim with us as Christians. That aim must be that the whole Church shall be brought to the highest possible completeness in Christ, that all the members of the mystical body should become vigorous and healthy, that the entire Church should be penetrated and filled with the divine life to utmost fullness. I am bold to say this is the longing desire and aim of every regenerate soul. Nothing is more certain than that things which tend to strife, and contention, and schism must hinder that aim. Can we doubt, with all the facts before us, that great evil has arisen from the spirit of separation which has been engendered and is assiduously cultivated among us? Is it to edification that a guild should be established on the profession of special attainments in grace? Does it improve the quality and usefulness of the class so distinguishing itself? Does experience prove that it is helpful to the body? Is it authorized by the teachings and spirit of the Master himself? It has appeared time and again: does the history of the past warrant the belief that it is of God? Is there not a better way? Reflect.

Brothers, God has taken us into a great fellowship, even the fellowship of himself; he has made us partakers of the divine nature; has given to us the spirit of his Son, the indwelling of the Holy Ghost; has raised us to sonship and heirship; has set us to be the lights of the world; to be co-workers with him in the salvation of our fellow-men; the custodians and dispensers of his eternal truth, and the witnesses of his grace to present and complete salvation from sin. This is our high-calling of God in Christ Jesus. We expect in a very brief period

to be done with this earthly life, and are confidently hoping to
be welcomed into heaven. In view of these things what manner of persons ought we to be? Surely we are called unto holiness. Let us not quibble and quarrel about names. The great thing is to live as children of the light. "We then, as workers together with him, beseech you also that ye receive not the grace of God in vain. . . . Giving no offense in any thing, that the ministry be not blamed; but in all things approving ourselves as the ministers of God, in much patience, in afflictions, in necessities, in distresses, in stripes, in imprisonments, in tumults, in labors, in watchings, in fastings; by pureness, by knowledge, by long suffering, by kindness, by the Holy Ghost, by love unfeigned, by the word of truth, by the power of God, by the armor of righteousness on the right hand and on the left, by honor and dishonor, by evil report and good report: as deceivers and yet true; as unknown, and yet well known; as dying, and, behold, we live; as chastened and not killed; as sorrowful yet always rejoicing; as poor, yet making many rich; as having nothing and yet possessing all things. O, ye [Christians]! our mouth is open unto you, our heart is enlarged. Ye are not straitened in us, but ye are straitened in your own bowels." "Finally, brethren, whatsoever things are true, whatsoever things are honest, whatsoever things are just, whatsoever things are pure, whatsoever things are lovely, whatsoever things are of good report; if there by any virtue, and if there be any praise, think on these things. Those things which ye have both learned, and received, and heard, and seen in me, do: and the God of peace shall be with you." "The very God of peace sanctify you wholly; and I pray God your whole spirit and soul and body be preserved blameless unto the coming of our Lord Jesus Christ." 2 Cor. vi, 1–12; Phil. iv, 8, 9; 1 Thess. v, 23. Let us heed these words of the great apostle, and, remembering

our great exampler, the Lord Jesus himself, let us as nearly as possible copy his example, and imitate his spirit, "who was holy, and harmless, and undefiled," and also "meek and lowly." God has entrusted us with a great trust: the blessed doctrine of Christian holiness. The trust puts us under peculiar responsibilities. Our fellow Christians of other communions have given no such hostages as we have. They are more modest in their professions. It is for us to prove that we are not rash, and by the beauty of our lives to furnish incentives to the higher experience which we profess. It is for all who profess the name of the Lord Jesus to depart from all iniquity, and to show themselves pure and spotless. Finally, brothers, have faith in God, pray earnestly and constantly for the heavenly help of the Holy Ghost, watch against the approaches of sin, abide near the cross. Keep a conscience void of offense toward God and man, be diligent, and so much the more as you see the day approaching. If these things are observed all men will know that you have been with Jesus. You will need no other testimony except as a grateful heart may move you to speak with meekness of the wondrous grace which saves you.

NOTE A.

Rev. Edward Everett Hale, D.D.,
Pastor of the South Congregational Church [Unitarian], Boston.

In answer to your note of October 5, let me say: 1. "Every person born in a Christian land is born a Christian, in a very familiar and legitimate sense of that word, precisely as every one born in America is born an American. The child is cared for by Christian skill, is fed on food which is Christ-given, is wrapped in a Christian blanket, and cannot escape from the beginning the influences of Christian life.

2. "I do not, however, suppose that it is in this sense of the word Christian that you put your question. I suppose that the answer which your question requires is that which the Saviour gave. He said, when he had occasion to answer it, 'Whosoever shall do the will of my Father who is in heaven, he is my brother, and sister, and mother.'"

This answer is as good now as it was then.

39 HIGHLAND STREET, ROXBURY, MASS.

Charles W. Eliot, LL.D.,
President of Harvard University.

In answer to your question of October 5, I beg to say that to my thinking he is a Christian who accepts Jesus Christ as the best moral and spiritual guide the world has seen, and tries in his Spirit to love and serve God and man.

CAMBRIDGE, MASS.

Rev. Cyrus A. Bartol, D.D.,
Pastor of the West Church [Unitarian], Boston.

To be a Christian is to live for others.

MANCHESTER, MASS.

Mrs. G. R. Alden ("Pansy"),
Author, Magazinist.

I very much regret that illness and an overwhelming pressure of work makes it impossible for me at this time to give a careful answer to the important question you ask, beyond the plain statement that, in my opinion, to be a Christian is to love the Lord Jesus Christ so much that I shall *desire* to have him reign supreme in my heart. I infer that you want this thought put into simpler, or rather into more detailed, language, and for that, as I said, I cannot secure the time.

WINTER PARK, FLA.

Rev. A. P. Peabody, D.D., LL.D.,
Professor of Christian Morals, Harvard University.

The Christian is he whose prime aim and evermore successful endeavor is Christ-likeness.

I know of no other definition which does not exclude some whom it ought to include, or include some who have no right to be called Christians.

11 QUINCY STREET, CAMBRIDGE, MASS.

Hon. Robert C. Pitman, LL.D.,
Judge of the Superior Court.

" What is it to be a Christian ? "

The simplest answer is the best. It is to be a disciple of Christ. Or, as Dr. Thomas Arnold puts it in one of his letters: "The purpose of his heart and mind is to obey and be guided by Christ, and therefore he is a Christian." This suffices for entrance upon the Christian life, and is the all-sufficient test of fellowship. The ultimate aim must be likeness to Christ.

NEWTON, MASS.

Mrs. Sarah K. Bolton,
Author, Writer.

Matt. vii, 12: "Therefore all things whatsoever ye would that men should do to you, do ye even so to them ; " *for Christ's sake.* Thus one leads an upright life from the best motive—unselfish love for another.

CLEVELAND, O.

Rev. David H. Moore, D.D.,
Editor of the *Western Christian Advocate.*

Building one's life upon the model—Christ Jesus.

CINCINNATI, O.

Rev. Howard Crosby, D.D., LL.D.,
Pastor of Fourth Avenue Church [Presbyterian], New York.

" What is it to be a Christian ? "

To be saved from sin and eternal death, faith in God as Saviour is the one essential. "None of them that trust in him shall be desolate (Hebrew "bear guilt,")—Psa. xxxiv, 22.

To be a Christian is to have this faith or trust in God, as made known in his Son Jesus Christ, the express image of his person.

116 EAST NINETEENTH STREET, NEW YORK.

Samuel Huntington, Esq.,

To *will* to *do* the will of God in the letter and spirit of 1 Cor. xiii and Gal. vi, 2.

BURLINGTON, VT.

Rev. O. P. Gifford, D.D.,
Pastor of the Warren Avenue Church [Baptist], Boston.

"What is it to be a Christian?"

In the parable of the sower Jesus pictures the Son of man sowing seed. The soil had not in itself the secret of a harvest, therefore culture of the soil could not bring a harvest. Bad soil was stony, or trodden hard, or thorn mortgaged, and gave no harvest even when the seed was offered; good soil depended upon seed brought to it and received by it for a harvest. A man becomes a Christian when he accepts the truth which Christ taught, co-operates with the truth received, yields his whole life to "the truth as it is in Jesus," and reproduces that life up to the measure of his ability, "some thirty, some sixty, and some a hundredfold." Capacity to reproduce varies, but "eternal life" depends upon acceptance of Christ, submission to Christ, co-operation with Christ, and reproduction of Christ
BOSTON, MASS.

Charles C. Bragdon,
Principal of Lasell Seminary.

Question: "What is it to be a Christian?"
Answer, brief and adequate: Mark i, 18.

To be a Christian seems to me to mean not necessarily to be a mature Christian. nor a faultless human being, but a *follower*. Better than all human comment is found in Matt. xx, 34, 27 and 28, and Matt. xxii, 37 and 39.
AUBURNDALE, MASS.

Mrs. Margaret Bottome,
President of the Order of King's Daughters.

"What is it to be a Christian?"

I answer: *To believe what Jesus Christ says, and to do what Jesus Christ tells us to do.* I remember hearing Mr. Moody tell of one who wanted to be a Christian, and he did all he could to show her the way; but no light, no joy, came to her. At last, in utter despair, he said, "Will you follow me in our Lord's Prayer, sentence by sentence?" So he commenced "Our Father"—and she repeated it after him until he reached the sentence, "forgive us our trespasses as we forgive those who trespass against us." She quietly said, "I never say that." "Why not?" said Moody. "Because there is a woman who injured me, and I never will forgive her." "Then," said he, "you will never become a Christian." "Well, here it ends," she said. And it did end in her going to the asylum in two years after. (May be it was called a case of religious insanity, but it was the want of it.) No, the time has come when we would better, with the life of our Lord in our hands, find out whether we are Christians or not. We will not need any formulated creed. Self-denial will take us a shorter way to becoming a Christian than any Shorter or Longer Catechism that I know anything about—the simple "follow Me," which means to us, *do* as I tell you. And the first thing he will tell us to do is to believe. He tells the truth when he says that God loves us and is our Father. The best and hardest thing is to really believe God is our Father.

And when we really say "*Father!*" we are Christians—not perfect Christians, but Christians. Our soldiers were as much in the army after they had taken the oath as they were when captains or generals.

Try this simple way! The oath is, "*I will obey Jesus Christ;*" and in less than five minutes you will be a Christian. Try it!

29 WASHINGTON PLACE, NEW YORK.

Rev. Lyman Abbott, D.D.,
Pastor of Plymouth Church and Editor of the *Christian Union*.

To be a Christian is, according to the New Testament phraseology, to be a follower of Christ—not to think something about him, but to appreciate him, love him, try to be like him, and trust in the help which comes through him for accomplishing the work which he gives his followers to do.

BROOKLYN, N. Y.

Professor David Swing, D.D.,
Pastor of the Independent Church, Chicago.

All those terms which end in "*nus*" in Latin and "*nos*" in Greek mean "belonging to." An Ameri*canus* is a man who belongs to America. This is the truest and sharpest meaning of Christia*nus* or Christian—a man, woman or child that belongs to Christ. The person who is like Christ in thought and deed, and who ardently wishes to become more and more like him, is the best Christian conceivable. As a Whig, or a Democrat, or a Republican may still be an American, so a Methodist, or a Baptist, or a Calvinist, may be a Christian. It is not necessary that a Christian should believe in any doctrines except those taught by Christ. He need not have Moses for a master. If necessary, he can live upon the Gospel of John or Matthew. Methodism or Calvinism does not harm him, but it is Christism that makes him and saves him.

403 SUPERIOR STREET, CHICAGO, ILL.

Rev. Theodore L. Cuyler, D.D.,
Pastor of the Lafayette Avenue Church [Presbyterian], Brooklyn.

"What is it to be a Christian?"

Jesus Christ answered this question when he said that whoever would be his disciple must deny himself and follow him. The man, therefore, who forsakes his sins, and by the help of the Holy Spirit endeavors to keep the commandments of his atoning Saviour and *Lord*, is a Christian. Faith *joins* the sinner's soul to the sinner's Saviour.

Mrs. Mary A. Livermore,
Lecturer, Author.

In late years, I have come to place great stress on life and character, as furnishing the best evidence of one being a Christian. "By their *fruits* ye shall know them."

And yet, it seems to me that a belief in the historic Christ, based on the New Testament histories, and illustrated and fortified by the researches of the reliable biblical scholars of the day, is essential, if one would be a well-grounded and intelligent Christian, theoretically.

Secondly: To this intellectual conviction must be added a persistent and courageous endeavor to act up to one's highest ideal, and to live a life of love to God and man, in accordance with the teachings of Christ. The life must be dominated by a high purpose,

> "To think, to feel, to do
> Only the holy Right;
> To yield no step in the awful race,
> No blow in the fearful fight."

One cannot be a Christian who does not aim to live among his fellows in love and helpfulness, bearing their burdens and illuminating their darkness. As the law of Christ's life was service to the world, so should it be that of those who call themselves by his name.

"By this shall all men know that ye are my disciples, if ye have love one to another."

MELROSE, MASS.

Rev. Charles Gordon Ames,
Pastor of the Church of the Disciples [Unitarian], Boston.

I respond to your request for an answer to the question, "What is it to be a Christian?" not without some reluctance, and not wholly to my own content; for behind every question lurk a hundred others, and who can voice the unspeakable? Words, too, are ambiguous and leaky; they never hold half one's meaning. All the same, I suppose we ought to keep on talking as the Spirit gives utterance to every man.

"What is it to be a Christian?"

We may be helped to an answer by the ideal "good man" described by Jesus—a man who "out of the good treasure of his heart bringeth forth good things," and who is thus known by his fruits to be a partaker of the divine nature. But a truly penitent sinner may also be called a Christian, as soon as his will goes over to the side of goodness. If I try to distinguish between the ordinary "good man" and the Christian, the latter presents himself as a *conscious* child of God, of the Christ pattern; that is, as one whose virtue is fashioned and colored by the Spirit of loving trust and obedience which we call *sonship*, of which brotherhood, justice, and willing service are the sure outcome. Technically, or according to the common use of language, the Christian is one who has reached this experience of sonship by the Christ-method, through the trusting surrender of self-will; or by heeding the counsels of perfection given and illustrated by Jesus, whose supreme sacrifice was simply the making of the Father's will his own. Faith, hope, love, pardon, the new life, regeneration—all inhere in this enthronement of the divine authority within the will.

But the name Christian is of secondary importance, and of ten definitions all may be true. One finds in the New Testament no exhortations to be "Christian;"

the whole urgency of the Gospel is to produce "sons of God" of such quality that the Father's life may be in them; that his Spirit may bear them witness, lead and sanctify them; and that the well-beloved may not be ashamed to call them brethren and joint-heirs with himself to the inheritance of love, wisdom, and power. We have many ways of talking about it; and spiritual experience has endless varieties; but all genuine goodness is of one stuff; and it never includes God's grace and man's freedom.
BOSTON, MASS.

Rev. Charles H. Parkhurst, D.D.,
Pastor of the Madison Square Church [Presbyterian], New York.

The following paragraph states as succinctly as I am able to do my conception of the essential fact in personal Christianity.

To be a Christian is humanly to incarnate the very life of God; and thus to be, in the strictest sense of the expression, a little Christ in our own little world.
133 EAST THIRTY-FIFTH STREET, NEW YORK.

Miss Frances E. Willard,
President of the National Woman's Christian Temperance Union.

"What is it to be a Christian?"

I have been trying to find out the answer to this most momentous question of all time for well-nigh fifty years! For, as one has said, the statements concerning Christ are of such a character that, if they are true, it matters very little what else is false; and if they are false, it matters very little what is true. The foundation-line of my character-pyramid is that they are as true, though not so demonstrable, as the proportions of geometry.

This granted, I should say that to be a Christian is to be adjusted to God's laws written in our minds, our members, and our spirits as accurately as the eye is adjusted to light, the ear to sound, the heart to love, the soul to faith. It is to have one's lifeship consciously guided by the Holy Spirit, God whispering his oracles through conscience, and to believe with one's inmost nature, intellect, sensibilities, and will that "God was manifest in the flesh, reconciling the world unto himself through Christ Jesus," our elder Brother, our Exemplar and Redeemer.
EN ROUTE IN NEW YORK.

Hon. Franklin Fairbanks,
President of Fairbanks Scale Company.

I could answer your inquiry at length, but to be very brief answer as follows: "What is it to be a Christian?"

To be a Christian is to believe on, and to follow, the Lord Jesus Christ, the Son of God, one of the Trinity. Acts viii, 37; John xi, 27.

To be a Christian one must have a change of heart, the "new birth." John iii, 3, 5.
ST. JOHNSBURY, VT.

Rev. A. J. Gordon, D.D.,
Pastor of the Clarendon Street Church, Baptist, Boston.

To be a Christian is one thing; to begin to be a Christian is quite another thing. The first attainment involves a life-time of toil and conflict and discipline; the second involves a surrender of the will to Christ. To believe on the Lord Jesus, which means to receive Christ as our personal Lord and Saviour, is the step by which we enter on the Christian life. In order that our faith may be proved to be sincere, it must be openly confessed. "If thou shalt confess with thy mouth the Lord Jesus, and believe in thy heart that God has raised him from the dead, thou shalt be saved." Rom. x. 9. This belief expressing itself in confession is that by which one begins to be a Christian; to be a Christian involves a whole succeeding life-time of obedience, cross-bearing, and holy living.

BOSTON, MASS.

Borden P. Bowne, LL.D.,
Professor of Philosophy, Boston University.

To be a Christian is to live in loving submission and active obedience to the will of God, trusting in his mercy in Jesus Christ.

BOSTON, MASS.

Mrs. Lucy Rider Meyer, M.D.,
Principal of the Chicago Training School, and Superintendent of the Chicago Deaconess Home.

To be a Christian is
1. Not to be a church member, though all Christians ought to be church members.
2. Not to be religious, though all Christians will be religious.
3. Not to "give one's body to be burned," though all Christians, by the grace of God, would, if need be, give their bodies to be burned.

To be a Christian is
1. To be born of God. "Except a man be born again, he cannot see the kingdom of God."
2. To be saved from sin. "Thou shalt call his name Jesus, for he shall save his people from their sins."
3. To be like Christ. "It is enough for the disciple that he be as his master."
4. To possess Christ. "He that hath the Son hath Christ."

CHICAGO, ILL.

Rev. Arthur T. Pierson, D.D.,
Editor of the *Missionary Review of the World*.

To be a Christian is to accept Jesus Christ as Saviour and Lord; as Saviour, to save from sin's penalty and power; as Lord, to rule over the heart and life. A Christian is, therefore, one who heartily believes on Jesus, and is therefore a follower of him.

PHILADELPHIA, PA.

Rev. Benjamin St. James Fry, D.D.,
Editor of the *Central Christian Advocate*.

To be a Christian is to obtain by faith in Christ the renewing and rectification of one's spiritual life, which life attains perfection in loving God with all the soul and mind and might and strength, and one's neighbor as one's self.

ST. LOUIS, MO.

Marion Harland,
Author, and Editor of the *Home-Maker*.

To be Christians is, first of all, believe, love, and trust in our crucified, risen, and ascended Lord and Saviour Jesus Christ, for our temporal salvation from sin, and eternal safety from the consequences of sin. As the fruit of this act of "saving faith," it follows that we should grow, daily, into likeness to him and nearness to him, looking to him for counsel, comfort, and strength. If we love him, we *will* keep his commandments. His Spirit informs the desires and shapes the actions of his true children. Thus springs into exercise the highest form of humanity. As he loved us, we must love also one another.

NEW YORK CITY.

Joseph Cook,
Lecturer, Author, Editor of *Our Day*.

A Christian is one who has obtained deliverance from both the love and the guilt of sin through the new birth and the atonement; one who has the faith that makes faithful; one who loves what God loves and hates what God hates : one who has gladly, affectionately, and irreversibly accepted God in Christ as both Saviour and Lord; one who sees God as Creator and Saviour so vividly and intelligently as to be willing to accept him as Ruler also; one who so beholds the cross of Christ that it is no cross to bear the cross.

BOSTON, MASS.

Rev. John P. Newman, D.D., LL.D.,
Bishop in the Methodist Episcopal Church.

You ask, "What is it to be a Christian?" There is a world of difference between a Christian and a Christ-like man. We count Christians by hundreds of millions, but the Christ-like people are reckoned only by millions. He who accepts Christ as "God manifested in the flesh;" his teachings as divine revelations to mankind; his ordinances of religion as the holiest obligations; his conditions of repentance, faith, conversion, as essential to eternal life; his claims on the love of the soul, the purity of the life, and on charity for man and devotion for God, is a Christian by profession of faith, as distinguished from all unbelievers whether in heathendom or Christendom. This is the honorable difference between the believer in the Lord and the Jew, the infidel and the pagan. Such are historical and doctrinal Christians, and the world is full of them. Let us believe that many such are beautiful in morality and lovable in philanthrophy. This is an immense power seen in governments, in systems of education, and in social reforms. All hail! to a power so potent and sublime! All this is the fruitage of a true professional conviction.

But there remains something deeper, broader, grander to be possessed. The measure of this better estate ranges from a desire to "flee from the wrath to come," to "all the mind that was in Christ," dominating the whole man, and an individual incarnation of Jesus, so that "Christ liveth in me." To cherish this desire by all possible means of grace, until all that is evil in us is eliminated, all that is good iu us is brought to maturity, and all that is lacking in us is supplied, is the duty and the privilege of each. Within these extremes are all true Christians. The "bruised reed" and the "smoking flax" are not to be despised. The "leaven in the meal" and the "mustard seed" in the earth are symbols of heavenly grace in the human heart. This is the babyhood of the Christian, lovable and beautiful as infancy. Beyond is the manhood, wherein the Christ-spirit holds every appetite and passion within the limits of law—purifies each motive, exalts each purpose, enonbles each aspiration, intones the conscience to the severest morality, enshrines the love of God and man in the "heart of hearts," and lifts up the human will and the divine will in their duality into a perfect oneness in our Lord.

Many have attained thereunto. They are walking in white; their conversation is in heaven. To them, prayer is the habit of the soul. Faith is the normal condition of the Spirit. Love is enthroned. O! that this experience may be my realized answer to your question, "What is it to be a Christian?"

NASHVILLE, TENN.

Rev. D. A. Whedon, D.D.,
Of the New England Southern Conference, Methodist Episcopal Church.

A Christian is one who believes and practices the truths and doctrines of Christianity, consisting of the facts of Christ's life and his teachings as found in the four gospels, and the doctrines based upon them by his apostles. One may, therefore, be a good Jew, a good Buddhist, a good Confucian, a good Mohammedan, or a good Agnostic, and be no Christian; for though he may believe some truths and practice some virtues which are taught by Christ, he rejects the Gospel and refuses supreme allegiance to him.

Christ's first teaching was to call to repentance; his second, the necessity of a new birth; his third, faith in himself as essential to salvation. The believing penitent God accepts, forgives, and brings into right relations to himself. By an inward supernatural change he makes the love of God the supreme affection of his soul and gives him power to refrain from sinning and to obey God. He also gives him a filial relation to himself, graciously adopting him as a child. The sinner thus becomes a Christian, and to continue a Christian he must continue what God has made him—forgiven, renewed, and his child.

A Christian, then, is one who takes Christ as his Saviour to save him and his Lord to rule him; who loves God more than all else, and his neighbor as himself; who, as to himself, subdues the evil within him; as to God, obeys his laws as given in the Scriptures; and as to his fellows, walks honestly, justly, unselfishly, kindly, helpfully, as Jesus would do in his place.

EAST GREENWICH, R. I.

www.ingramcontent.com/pod-product-compliance
Lightning Source LLC
Chambersburg PA
CBHW020846160426
43192CB00007B/810